PARENTING A TEENAGER
Copyright © 2017 by **Dr. Funmi Oboye**

ISBN: 978-1-944652-45-6
Published By:
Cornerstone Publishing
A division of Cornerstone Creativity Group LLC
+1 516-547-4999
Info@thecornerstonepublishers.com
www.thecornerstonepublishers.com

This publication may not be reproduced, stored in a retrieval system, or transmitted in whole or in part, in any form or by any means, electronic, mechanical, photocopying, recording, or otherwise, without the prior written permission of the publisher

All rights reserved.
Printed in United States of America

DEDICATION

This book is dedicated to my children and their spouses; my teenage students in all the secondary schools where I had worked and the teenagers whom I now have the priviledge of raising through the instrumentality of my NGO - Engr. Timothy Tonloju Adesubokan Memorial Foundation .

Thank you very much for your encouragement and support, always. I love you all.

ACKNOWLEDGEMENT

I appreciate the power of enablement, wisdom and drive given to me by God to write this book in my plight to ensure that "Teenage children" are strategically and patiently handled by their parents, guardians, teachers and all other adults around them, so that they can be great achievers indeed, much more than the Biblical David, Joseph and Daniel.

As a Parent, Teacher, Principal, Educational Administrator and Educational Consultant charged mainly with the responsibility of shaping the lives of children at home and in various secondary schools in the education sector where I had worked consistently for over three decades, till now, I have been able to categorically outline how best to discharge the Divine duty of parenting teenagers to their ultimate advantage and to the glory of God.

My husband, Engr. Olaitan, Femi Oboye was very supportive of my move to write this book, which I believe will serve as a compendium of practical solutions to the challenges of parenting the teenage child adequately, in these days of stiff economic strive for financial attainment, by parents .

My children; students in all the various secondary schools where I had worked over the years; the beneficiaries of my NGO who are teenagers, must be commended for providing themselves to me, for a continuous "teaching practice" on the subject of "parenting a teenager adequately", which had afforded me the opportunity of writing this laudable book, so that parents of teenage children can be guided in the discharge of this divine duty of parenting aright, as co-creators with God. He created them and sent them to us to complete the process, with His wisdom available for our use, in carrying out this special assignment.

My appreciation also goes to Mrs. L.B. Olaleye, who proofread the book for me. God will be there for you too in all situations ma; my only biological sister Bose, you are highly treasured by God.

I also commend parents who are committed to their parenting duties, in its totality. Please keep it up. The children actually belong to God, one day they will be in their respective homes as parents too. They are God's heritage, we are just stewards for Him. We will not lose our reward from God over this unique venture.

Finally, I acknowledge the dexterity of all those who assisted me in the production of this book from one stage to the other. I say a **BIG THANK YOU,** to all of you.

Dr (Mrs) Funmi Oboye
August, 2014

FOREWORD

I consider it a great honour to write the foreword of a book whose author is a blessing to the education industry.

Funmi Oboye is a consistent, devoted and passionate educationist who has helped in shaping the lives of many teenagers who passed through her hands at the Federal Government College, ljanikin, Lagos; Queens College, Yaba, Lagos; University of Lagos International School. Akoka, Lagos, and many reputable private secondary schools where she had worked as Principal and Educational Administrator. She has had the grace of God following her, everywhere she served.

She has a unique way of handling the pre-teens and teenagers whom she raised, which positively affected their destinies.

This book will go a long way in providing parents of teenagers and all other adults around our teenagers in getting the parenting of this unique age of children right.

It is written from the perspective of an experienced parent of teenagers, who had been in the midst of teenagers in the church, school and at home. She said that "It has been a pleasant experience gathered by her over the years that she would want to share with parents whose children are currently in the teenage age bracket."

Some parents whose children are teenagers now, still treat them like children and this has resulted into the insubordination of such children and caused some uproar for them in the school, with teachers and at home with their parents.

This book serves as guide to parents in the discharge of this divine duty of leading these young adults in the right path of life, practically, for a successful journey to the right destination of success and excellent attainment in life.

It is highly recommended for your reading pleasure and a tum around in your parenting style in the interest of the children, and our nation to the glory of God.

Mr. Yinka Abiodun
President, Lake Point Education Institute,
Gbagada, Lagos
2014.

PREFACE

I give God the glory for the priviledge He has given me to operate for over thirty years now in the midst of teenagers as a Parent, Counselor, Teacher, Principal, Educational Administrator and an Educational Consultant.

It has given me a clear insight into the lives of teenagers. I have found them to be unique, indeed.

At the teenage stage of life, the children are passing through a process of maturing into adulthood. So, they can be referred to as" Adults in training." Parents, guardians, teachers and other adults around them have the mandate from God to train, nurture and mould them to become matured, sophisticated, dependable and responsible adults, because we had passed through the way of life, these teenagers are just passing through.

This book outlines the characteristics of teenagers, their likes and dislikes; how to counsel them adequately, how to penetrate their world and get them willingly impacted.

It is a guide to the right way to parent a teenager with an accompanied far reaching success, required by every stakeholder.

Some of the teenagers parented by single parents, go through some unannounced trauma and psychological disturbance, as a result of the situation they found themselves in, while their parents are usually completely unaware of it. The details of how such teenagers can be parented adequately, are analyzed in this book, in order to ensure that their destinies are actualized with ease.

This book is a "must read" for every adult. It is especially recommended to Parents, Guardians, teachers, Guidance Counselors and every adult who is set to impact the teenagers around him/her absolutely, and able to adequately fulfill the divine assignment of parenting them for the attainment of an all-round excellent life and living, now and in the future.

Dr (Mrs) Funmi Oboye
August, 2014

CONTENT

DEDICATION ii

ACKNOWLEDGEMENT iii

FOREWORD v

PREFACE vii

Chapter ①
Teenagers and their Parents 1

Chapter ②
True Life Stories of the adverse effect of Neglecting a Teenage Child As revealed by some of them I encountered 7

Chapter ③
A few more Examples to make the Picture more Clearer 17

Chapter ④
Significant features of the Teenage or Adolescent Child 23

Chapter ⑤
Teenagers Believe that They are Adults Too 27

Chapter ⑥
The Psychology And Physiology of the Teenage Development to Adulthood 33

Chapter ⑦
Further Strategies for the Parenting Of Teenagers 39

Chapter ⑧
Good Relationship with GOD is Non-negotiable 45

Chapter ⑨
How to Draw the line as a Parent 49

Chapter ⑩
Self Esteem and how it Affects Teenagers 53

Chapter 11
The Uniqueness Teenage Children 67

Chapter 12
Personality Types of our Children (Pre-Teens/Early Teens) and Academic Work 75

Chapter 13
Counselling your Children Effectively – The Teenagers and the Younger Ones 83

Chapter 14
The Teenage Children from Single Parent Homes and how to Raise Them 93

Chapter 15
The Various Experiences of Teenagers from single parent homes in school 97

Chapter 16
Tips That Could Guide You The Single Parent of a Teenager .. 117

Chapter 17
Relating with Teenagers from Single Parent Homes by their Parents 127

Chapter 18
Teenagers Can be Amazingly Extra-ordinary, If Given the Chance 133

ABOUT THE AUTHOR 143

Chapter 1
Teenagers and their *Parents*

Who is a teenager?

They are children or young adults of ages 13 to 19 years old, who are usually of secondary school and university age group. Statistics have shown that they make up about 55% of the world's population.

Parenting of a child at any level is a divine duty which must be carried out with all commitment and diligence. This is because, if it is not done adequately, it will thwart the destiny of the individual child, affect the lives of the parents, siblings and others in the society as a whole.

An ill-parented teenage child is a menace to everyone around him/her and everyone who gets in contact with him/her. They are the ones who eventually become prostitutes, robbers, area boys/girls, cult members, thugs, rapists, abductors, swindlers etc.

The teenage stage of life is one in which every parent must be poised for a successful performance. Once the child is neglected by the parents or guardians at their stage, by abandoning their parental duties to the school alone or to nobody at all, the harm is done forever. The University or Polytechnic will be the next expected environment for a child after his/her secondary education but alas, the job of reformation of character is expected to have been completed in the final year of the secondary school, in the lives of the children by the teachers in school and the parents/guardiansat home. The place of worship of the parents also have a part to play in it.

The under-graduates on the University campus are believed to be young adults who can take care of themselves and know what they want out of life, so, nobody guides them on a day to day basis as **it** was the case when they were in the Primary and Secondary Schools. Hence, a student in the University can choose to read or not to read; he decides on whether to attend lectures or not. He takes his decision on several issues of life, whether good or bad without being monitored by anybody, especially in Federal and State Universities. However, in Private Universities, they are still being monitored to some extent, but where the student has proved incorrigible or far below average academically, whether in a State, Federal or Private University, he will be expelled and thereafter he will be referred to as a drop-out. He will then join the group of people who constitute a big hazard to the development and welfare of their environment. Such an individual becomes useless to himself, his parents/sibling, his society, nation and God. His destiny becomes thwarted and unrealizable just because of the carelessness, ignorance and non-challance of those in whose custody God had placed him. We must not give the excuse that he refused to take correction that must be because the correction started too late.

I usually pause to appreciate parents who had embraced their divine duty of parenting with all seriousness, not allowing their jobs or other personal pursuits to hinder them from making the best of it. They have sacrificed time, money, pleasure and leisure for it so that they can enjoy a peaceful old age, wholesome family and life in general.

On the contrary, those who have failed to parent their teenage children adequately have created a lot of confusion and pandemonium for their respective families, environment, nation and the world at large because such children will eventually become useful vessels in the hands of the devil to perpetrate all forms of evil, menace and confusion as being experienced in several nations of the world now.

They have not been taken through the rudiments of good behavior by anybody and wherever they go to, they are attracted to people like them in order to continue with the atrocities they have been used to.

Some parents/ guardians think they can get a teenage child who had become completely wayward and bad easily reformed. The only period we can affect the life of a child positively with ease is from infancy to the pre-teenage age i.e. age 12 years old. As from age 13 years old and above, depending on the environment and parenting style, it becomes more difficult for the child to be reformed. Reformation, then depends on prayers, God's intervention, counseling and love. Canning, shouting, punishment will not solve the problem at all. It will only get the child more hardened and determined to get worse as his own way of hitting you back.

As teenagers, any unfriendly method of reformation will not work. This is because at that age, they want to know why you want them to carry out your instructions especially as they have a different perception of life. They can't see what you regard as bad in the same light as you. This is because in this phase of life, they are in a world of their own and you have to be diplomatic in handling them. They can see what you don't see yet. Honesty is desired, because, they can't be deceived.

Please note the following about the 3 phases of Parenting:
- (a) Ages 5-11 years old is the training stage
- (b) Ages 12 to 14 years is the coaching stage
- (c) Ages 15 to 19 years and above is the friendship stage. This is how it is psychologically.

If the adults in their lives had positioned themselves as their friends when they were growing up, they would have believed in them early enough in life and agree with whatever corrections they are making believing that they mean well for them, that is why as parents and guardians you must take your parenting duties serious from the onset.

Teenagers have a world of their own and only their friends are allowed in. Adults who are not their friends are seen as intruders and bullies who just want to get them demoralized because they are older. They will not tell you all these but they will act it out. However, if you were close to them when they were infants, right on to the teenage age, they will not think that way.

So, move very close to your child as from infancy through to the teenage stage to adulthood so that he/ she does not get derailed, and become a source of concern to you instead of being a source of joy.

If you fail to move very close to your teenage child with the desired love, care and concern for his future and ensure that he gets actualized and fulfill his destiny, someone else will fill the vacuum and the person might be someone who will influence him negatively and it will be too late for you to retrieve his life and destiny back.

This is now much more necessary than ever before in these days of social media where he can pick a lot of negative things on line without your knowledge, even without leaving home, we must not joke with our parenting duties, especially in times like these.

I have been privileged to witness the expulsion of some students in several secondary schools where I taught and headed as a Principal, situations where the parents of the children who had proved very notorious and incorrigible would vouch for the innocence of their children until we provide them with all proofs and evidence of their negative attitudes and behavior that had proved beyond every reasonable doubt that they should not be allowed to continue to interact with well behaved and innocent children so that they would not influence them negatively. The obvious fact was that their parents didn't know them; they just lived in the same house with them like strangers. Incidentally, many s are like this today.

Chapter ②

True Life Stories of the adverse effect of Neglecting a

Teenage

Child

As revealed by some of them I encountered.

To buttress the point I raised about parents of teenage children who did not know the atrocities perpetrated by their children and the extent they could go, I will site some true life examples here, but the names of the characters I will mention are ficticious but the stories are events that really happened.

(a) A boy, Segun was caught smoking at the back of the school fence. He was a day student from Junior Secondary One to Senior Secondary Two, so that he will be able to concentrate more on his studies and make very good grades in his final exams in SS3 which is the final year in a secondary school, his parents sent him to the boarding house. Segun was used to smoking but the parents never knew that he was a cigarette smoker. They owned their business and they usually left home at 7am and would arrive at 9pm every day. They had the habit of travelling out of the country with their children during their holidays, but they did not really know what the children were capable of doing. According to the school's rules and regulations, as contained in the Students Handbook, the penalty for smoking was immediate expulsion.

When his parents were invited and informed, they were surprised that he could do such a thing. They wondered where he had learnt how to smoke especially as nobody was a smoker in the family.

When the boy was interrogated by me in a friendly manner; in order to know how he could be assisted to turn a new leaf despite the expulsion from school, since that would not be the end of his life.

In most cases, parents abdicate their parental responsibilities to their domestic staff, hence the lopsided upbringing, simply because you can't give what you don't have. A Security man, your driver, house girl, house boy or any domestic staff of yours can never parent your child adequately no matter how well behaved you think such a domestic staff is.

> (c) A boy, Richard was caught with another student's laptop stolen by him. The owner of the laptop had searched everywhere for it for over six months without being able to find it. Richard thought the owner would have forgotten about it. He defaced the laptop to a large extent, especially the exterior part of it, believing that it could not be recognized as the lost laptop; he scribbled his name on it and took it to school. The owner of the laptop saw it and was still able to identify some signs in some corners of the laptop as a clear proof that it was his own. Richard was caught red-handed as a thief.

During the process of interrogation, it was discovered that his father lived permanently outside the country while his mother with whom he lived in Nigeria, ran a business that requires incessant travelling to different parts of the world. In most cases, she would be away for six months at a stretch, leaving Richard and his two other brothers who were all teenagers at home, believing that they were old enough to take care of themselves. The Security man was given the mandate to oversee their movement and welfare.

If the mother had been in, I'm sure she would have raised an alarm and insisted the laptop which was not his own should be returned to the owner especially as he had his own too. Richard would also have picked up some other nefarious habits and later become an ardent criminal without the knowledge of his parents due to the abandonment of their Divine parental responsibility to the Security man.

A teenage child can be a good pretender before a parent who is a stranger to him, a parent who is too strict on him and a parent whom he had concluded that he could not satisfy. If a child does not feel loved by the parents, he or she will seek for love elsewhere. Many affected teenagers who found themselves in such a dilemma, had become cult members, prostitutes and criminals of all sorts in an attempt to seek for love. They got the love they desired from wrong sources where they became robed in, with the wrong set of people.

(d) Biodun, a teenager, whose age was 14 years old at the time of this incident had parents who were both business people. They would leave home in the morning, as early as 7:00am and come back at 10:00pm every day except on Sundays. He had two senior brothers as well. Whenever they were back from school, several girls who were their school mates visited them and they were always having sexual relationships with them. Nobody was ever around to check them, neither did their parents knew anything about it. This continued for a long time until one evening when the mother of a girl who was 12 years old, Lizzy in JS3 accosted Biodun's parents in the company of her daughter whom she claimed was 6months pregnant for their son, Biodun who was the ninSSl.

Biodun's parents disagreed at first and refused to accept the allegation. Lizzy's parents took the matter to court while Biodun's parents too got their Lawyer to defend the case, because they thought that they were sure of the innocence of their son. The court directed that they should go for the DNA test to verify the ownership of the expected baby. The case turned out to be in favour of Lizzy's parents. Biodun was the authentic father of the baby. His parents were disappointed and Biodun too was ashamed of himself but alas, he became a father at the age of 14 years old. Immediately the school authority was aware of it, they were both expelled.

The list is endless but I will endeavour to add a few examples later for clarity. True life stories of where some teenage children had missed their ways in life because of parental abandonment as a result of a desperate pursuit for money or being engulfed by their careers, ambition and businesses to the detriment of the adequate parenting of their teenage children. Such parents end up biting their fingers later when any remedy will no longer be applicable. So, now is the time for us as parents to sit up in order to avoid the doom and the biting of fingers at old age.

If the necessary amendment is not done in time and the child leaves home for the University campus, he will be attracted to people like him and end up being a cult member and for the girls, they pursue and befriend men who are old enough to be their fathers for the sake of sexual embellishment (because they are used to having sex indiscriminately and spending money recklessly without working for it) while their parents are too busy to attend to their parental duties of bonding, nurturing and raising their children.

Some parents think parenting is just about providing for the needs of the children alone. It is part of it but it is definitely much more than that.

A friend of mine, a University lecturer, told me that her father was never at home when she was growing up with her siblings but he was providing everything they needed except his presence, which they considered vital to their adequate development psychologically, spiritually and mentally - (these are the main essence of an individual's personality and make-up) They missed the warmth, counsel, nurturing and pampering of the God-figure in the lives.

She said one day her siblings and herself summoned their father to a meeting by writing an official letter of protest to him and they also insisted on having a meeting with him on a date they stated there and the venue as well, in order to air their views about the matter and give him a piece of their minds.

The meeting was held, during which the children, one after the other expressed their appreciation and gratitude to God who had given them such a rich and comfortable father who could provide for all their needs but they emphasized that they had always felt like children from a single parent home where only their mother was around to bring them up. They appealed to him in tears, rolling on the floor, begging him to please complete the process of parenting by making available his presence with them, even if it will be just one whole day of the week on a consistent basis, when they could discuss with him intimately, as friends and have feelings of having a father, as well.

The father who had hitherto kept on saying that "I was always going out to get some money, so as to fend for my family," realized the need for his presence with his children, in addition to providing for their needs. She said since then, their father started making out time out of his very busy schedule, to interact with his children not only as a father but also as a friend. The testimony was that, he told them later that he was making more money than he made before he started incorporating them into his weekly schedule. I believe that it is because, God who is the one who prospers and who also gave their father the duty of parenting, decided to bless him more with less struggles because he was obedient to Him (God) by parenting his children adequately because that is God's desire.

Repudiation or abandonment of parental duties for any reason tantamonts to telling God who gave you the task that you don't have time for Him and His work and that He (God) should leave you alone. Let us always remember that these children did not beg us to give birth to them, we offered to do so on our own volition and if we fail to parent them adequately and sacrificially, thereby ruining their lives and thwarting their destinies due to our own carelessness, selfishness and ignorance, we will pay for it here on earth and stand before God to give an account of why He must not punish us for it. It is a whole life and destiny ruined, which would have been saved from ruins.

WHY THE RAT RACE?

We should remember that there will be a time when we will be too old to take care of ourselves, no matter how rich we may be (we all pray to live up to a ripe old age). It is the type of children you have brought up that will determine the type of parents you will have then. If as a result of your non-challance and always away from your children, they have become very untrusted and undependable, once they know you have any money somewhere in the house, they will arrange for how you will be robbed. We have heard of stories where children arranged for the abduction of their parents in order to get some money out of the venture.

The Old man and his family

The story was told by an old man whose wife was late and the children were very wayward. He remarried after the wife died but alas, his sons were having sexual relationship with his wife until she became pregnant and there was a controversy as regards the paternity of the child - could it be the father or his sons who had become a nuisance to him because even at their age of 40 years old and 38 years old respectively, they were still living in their father's house with their respective families. After he died, there was a lot of controversy over his property and court cases started, among the children tussling for the ownership of his property.

This type of situation occurs in some families in various parts of the world. I am sure that nobody ever prays for such. The antidote to ensure a diligent and committed parenting of our children especially the teenage ones is to be there for them in all ramification. If they leave home for the University as disciplined children who know what they want out of life, they will attract others like them over there and be successful all the way.

On the other hand, if a teenage child leaves home for the University as an indisciplined person who has no goals or aspiration and who is a stranger to you as his parents, anything can happen on the campus. In several cases, teenagers who left home for the University campus as indisciplined, will definitely attract indisciplined friends like themselves. The possibility of becoming a 419 person i.e. fraudulent, perpetrators of cyber crimes, cult members, sugar daddy girls on campus, and undergraduates with several criminal tendencies, is very high. This is because parents do not need to visit University undergraduates as often as they were visited when they were in the boarding houses in their secondary school days.

Ideally, a University undergraduate should be matured enough to take care of himself at that level.

We must ensure that we parent and nurture them to the optimum at the secondary school level; otherwise, it can be disastrous. Once they miss the right nurturing and adequate upbringing at the secondary school level, only God's intervention can ever make it right again.

Chapter ③
A few more
Examples
to make the
Picture more Clearer

A girl, Vic, whose mother Mrs. Regina John was a big time business woman, who was never at home and always travelling out of the country to purchase goods from England, United States, Japan and Turkey. She had her warehouse in different major cities of Nigeria. Mr. David John, her husband was based in the U.K. Her mother, (Mrs. John's mother) was the one parenting Vic and her brothers (3 of them). They all lived in their very big and sophisticated mansion in Victoria Island. In order to make the work easier for the old woman who was about 75 years old, two house boys, a house girl, one Nanny, a security man, were all employed as the domestic staff of the family. They all lived within the four walls of the mansion.

Children can't parent themselves

All the amenities were highly dignifying and commendable, but the physical presence and commitment of the parents themselves was very necessary for the proportionate growth and development of the children. God did not create children to parent themselves, He knew that they would not be able to do it effectively without the full participation of the biological parents and the adults around them, for a meaningful development hence whenever children are at home, parents are expected to be in charge of raising them; in school, their teachers take over, in the school bus, while coming home - the school bus driver and the bus assistants move into the parenting arena for them. Those who are picked home after school by their parents' drivers, between the school and the home, the driver takes over as a parent; for those who usually go home on their own, there will be a public transportation driver to pick them with several adults en-route as they go home. The adults around them then, will perform the necessary parental duty.

This is God's ordained plan for parenting. No vacuum should be allowed until when the child is 19 or 21 years old depending on the culture, during which the result of your parenting exercise over the child will be visibly seen by all and sundry. This will be reflected in the child's behavior and way of life in general.

Parents must be prepared to sacrifice enough quality time in interacting with their children. It is not just about your presence with him at home but real interaction as friend with friend. Real intimacy with him will give you the opportunity of full mentorship.

Without the knowledge of the parents Vic became pregnant thrice and aborted

Vic's parents did not know that the Security man, Abu and one of the house boys, Akpan, were always having sexual relationship with Vic. She became pregnant about three times even at her tender age, since both men knew that they were both involved, they contributed some money and took her to a Doctor for abortion on each occasion. The parents got to know later about her illicit affairs with the men.

Akpan and Abu were immediately sacked and they employed two other men who were believed to be disciplined and diligent, as replacement. It has been observed and proved that sexual relationship after marriage as ordained by God solidifies the relationship. The couple get to love each other more as they engage in it. This is more pertinent on the part of the man to his wife. If it is practiced before marriage, the partners become so engrossed in it and they will sometimes have a strong urge to have it, but for a married person, he simply meets the wife on bed and vice versa.

A FEW MORE EXAMPLES TO MAKE THE PICTURE MORE CLEARER

An unmarried person who has started having sex before marriage, will not mind meeting anybody once the urge is physiologically there. In most cases, they will just jump into bed with anything in skirt or trousers. It is only God's intervention in such a life that can stop such an immoral act, once they start if off, hence God had ordained that it should be done only after marriage. Vic got to this point of no return in her sexual life. So, she ended up becoming pregnant again within two years interval, this time the pregnancy belonged to the senior brother of her friend in school who was in the senior secondary school of another school, different from the one she was attending with the sister of the boy.

Her class teacher Mrs. Christie Agu was the one who discovered and she reported the matter officially to the school authority. Her parents were invited to school. They could not respond to the invitation because they were both outside the country as at then. The girl was expelled from school with immediate effect and that was the end of her secondary school career in that school. She was then in SS2 i.e., senior secondary School year two and she was fourteen years old. The parents finally returned home and decided that she was not going to abort, not knowing that their daughter had had three abortions already.

The mother sent her to the house of a friend of her's who lived in another part of the country, a place where nobody knew her. She stayed there until she delivered the baby who was brought home with her. The family Nanny started nursing the baby. Vic resumed back to another school to continue with her studies. The boy who pregnated her accepted the paternity of the baby but was also a student at that time. His parents simply told Vic's parents that the young man, Ezekiel will take up the full paternal responsibility whenever he starts earning a salary.

To everybody's utmost shock and dismay, Vic was found pregnant again while in her final year in the secondary school. This time, the pregnancy was for Ezekiel's best friend Ola, who blatantly denied the paternity of the expected baby. One would have thought that after the pregnancy that led to the expulsion of Vic from school, the parents would have amended their schedule to accommodate a time of interaction with their children but they said it was not possible for them to do so because according to them they will need to go on with their businesses at the same tempo in order to be able to provide adequately for the needs of the family. Many parents who are like minded will think the same way. My question is "why did they give birth to those children when they knew that they would be too busy to parent them.

However, they might be right but it should not be done at the detriment of the children. Can you imagine a case like that? For a girl below the age of 15 years old to have had two children for two men even before having any academic certificate and unmarried. What an embarrassing situation and the truncating of a destiny all due to parental negligence!!!

Parents should learn from this and not learn from experience. It is a general saying that "experience is the best teacher, but the school fees can be very expensive to pay" because many things would have been destroyed without remedy in the school of "Mr. Experience" so, it is safer to learn from other people's experiences than to experience it yourself especially if the situation is a negative one. Inside every teenager, there is a giant, a hero, a helper and a genius and even then, they still need our help, guidance and nurturing.

Chapter 4
Significant features of the Teenage or Adolescent Child

It is very important for parents with teenage children to know them intimately in order to know what to expect of them. The prevalence of the following features in a teenager depends on the level of maturity, exposure and adequate parenting of the individual child from the infancy. Some, if not all can be found in each of them.

(a) **They confront the adult world.**
The respect they used to have for adults diminishes and deviant attitude appears. This is because it becomes obvious to them that adults are not as perfect as they had thought.

(b) **They can be argumentative**
They develop a rapidly growing thought process, as a result of which they are able to present logical arguments and end up beating their opponents successfully. This "intellectual" process is often resented by parents because they now see themselves as being deprived of the ability to persuade their children. At this level, parents are to discuss things over with them and let them know clearly, the positive and negative effects of issues; otherwise, they will think that you are simply interested in imposing your authority on them because you are older than them. They will then look for a way of rebelling as their own way of hitting back at you.

(c) **It is a period of "high sensitivity"**
They have a suspicious attitude towards parents and all other adults around them. They believe that adults Are always interested in dominating them. If such a feeling is allowed to continue, there will be a break down in relationship. They should be allowed to know, in details, why they are being corrected on any issue. Give a clear and transparent explanation for any action of yours that has to do with them. Be very honest in your dealings

with them. They can't be easily deceived; they can read in-between-the lines. Make sure that they believe in you otherwise, they will never "take you serious," but once they believe in you, it will be very easy for you to handle them because they will not want to offend you.

(d) **They hardly hold a realistic self-concept**
They have a higher concept of who they are than who they actually are. On the other hand, sometimes it dawns on them that they are young and some other times, they have a strong feeling that they are adults (it is a process of growth and it is psychological).

In order to help them grow up and get matured fast enough, treat them like adults. Respect their opinions, relate to them as friends and whenever you need to be firm on them, do so with some tenderness and explain to them why you just must be firm on them at that point. Let them know that you are doing so, in their own interest. They will willingly learn the lesson and obey without any grudge. It will enable them to be able to mentor their peers who might not have the priviledge of the right tutelage they have been opportuned to have. If you think that you owe them no explanation whenever you punish them, they can become hardened but pretend in your presence so as to avoid the punishment and continue with the bad behavior in your absence.

(e) **They hate insincerity and inconsistency**
Parents must be honest and transparent when dealing with them. They close their ears to advise and open their eyes to example. They emulate their parents and all other adults around them. It is necessary for parents to have clear rules for them and let them know that the obedience of each of the rules is in their own interest.

Chapter ⑤

Teenagers
Believe that They are
Adults
Too

As young adults, they do not want to be handled like children. This must be understood by every parent s young adults, they do not want to be handled like and adults around them for effective parenting.

If they are handled like children, by parents who are oblivious of the fact of their daily growth into adulthood, they might be forced into a rebellious state, depending on the existing relationship between them and such parents. If a friendly relationship had existed from a younger age, they will easily comply, especially if their views are also respected even if it is occasional, if not, he will find it repulsive and he might rebel.

They believe that they should not be over-controlled by the adults around them. They prefer to be handled with respect as adults-in-training as they are concerned, they have to be recognized and respected too by the adults around them.

SOME CHARACTERISTICS OF THEIR REBELLIOUS STATE

(a) Unaccepted mode of dressing
(b) Secrecy beyond measure
(c) Illegal relationship
(d) Use of lewd and obscene languages
(e) Use of coated languages
(f) Yieldedness to peer pressure
(g) Deviation from family, school or societal norms
(h) Truancy
(i) Ganging up
(j) Hanging out with friends
(k) Refusal to have the same spiritual belief with parents
(l) Changing of place of worship
(m) Refusal to copy notes or submit assignments
(n) Deliberate disrespect to constituted authority

In a situation where parents are strangers to their teenage children, there is a high possibility of peer pressure on the child and a negative influence on the child's behavior and attitude to life. This is to be expected. If parents are very friendly with them, they are likely to discuss various challenges that would have resulted into peer pressure or social media moral issues with them during a close interaction with dad or mum, and he will be adequately mentored and counseled against any negative behavior. They will enable him see the negative consequences of such an act on his destiny; academic work; social life; spiritual life and his future. He will immediately correct himself such a handling will enable him to assume the position of a mentor to his mates, friends and acquaintances.

Teenagers, agree with the counsel or advice of whosoever they believe in and ignore that of anyone they do not believe in, no matter how superior that person's advice may be. So as parents, it is our duty to ensure that they believe in us. Let's note that it is psychological, so, it can't be enforced. If your seemingly over scheduled duties had led to the abandonment of your interaction with them, they will believe more in their friends or your domestic staff than you, whether those ones are right or wrong, they will carry out their directives and act to please them. They will refer to the counsel and advice of their parents as "Old School" but it could also be the other way round if they believe in you. In such a situation, when they meet with a set of friends, classmates, or other peers in general, who believe contrary to whatever you have told them was right, they will uphold your views and ensure they believe in it, if they refuse, they will part ways with them. They will ensure that they move with only good friends who will live up to expectation, based on the continuous tutelage of their parents.

They will continue to live a disciplined life wherever they find themselves, even in your absence.

LET US LOOK AT SOME OTHER VISIBLE TRAITS OF REBELLION IN TEENAGERS.

Causes of wild and rebellious behaviour in teenagers:

The behavioral patterns analyzed here are usually exhibited by teenagers who are emotionally disturbed i.e. they have one major problem or the other that must be diagonised psychologically and treated by the parents themselves by way of counseling for the purpose of adjustment. Once the cause of the wild behavior is detected, the child can be assisted to come out of it. If the problem diagnosed is very serious, a specialist counselor can be contacted for a solution out of such a psychological state.

Several things can be responsible for such a wild behavior e.g.

(a) Repetition of class

(b) Unhappy state of parents at home

(c) Disorders at home, school or dormitory that affect the well being of the child.

(d) Prolonged deprivation of any sort that affects the child psychologically.

(e) Loss of a parent or sibling

(£) The long absence of a dearly beloved parent from home

(g) Being exposed to a situation which the child considers disgraceful.

When they act out their feelings under the above-mentioned conditions, They are considered rebellious.

(h) A poor relationship with parents - rules and regulations at home without any close relationship with them can lead to rebellion. Parents are to ensure that they establish a really close relationship with their teenage children before the rules are stated or reeled out otherwise it will lead to an outward or inward rebellion. They might appear to be obedient while they are actually nursing some grudges against the parents because they will be feeling oppressed and intimidated especially as the parent has not taken time to let them know why those rules must be obeyed in their own interest. It can also lead to a low self esteem.

(i) Rebellion expressed by a teenager could be an effort to communicate his feelings and resentment. A child was quoted to have told the parents that nobody takes him serious at home until he forces his feelings on them.

(j) It could be a means of seeking control over their lives. They might respond positively to appropriate parental guidelines and boundaries, but once they feel that their parents control everything about their lives as if they are children, they attempt to shed off the control by breaking the rules or control. If their parents attempt to exert more control through threats, coercion or physical restrain, they then pause to take a decision as regards whether to rebel or give in. They can do any of the two.

(k) A lack of boundaries and expectations - in permissive homes, where there are no boundaries or high moral expectations, the child may be rebellious as a result of lack of training or improper upbringing, especially because he has no values or principles to guide him.

(l) Rebellion could be an expression of anger, aggressiveness or deprivation; such a child will be exhibiting a bottled up emotion and can "explode" anytime in a surprising manner.

Other causes of rebellion include:

(a) When parents are too strict, children rebel in order to draw attention to the fact that they are growing up and should not be treated like children.

(b) If parents are inconsistent in their approach in handling the children, they will cease to take them serious.

(c) If parents are rigid, the children may become rebellious. As the children grow up, there is need to become more flexible as parents. If parents refuse to treat them like young adult despite the children's rebellious state, they will become notorious and continue to misbehave continuously as their own way of hitting back.

Chapter 6
The Psychology And Physiology of the Teenage Development to Adulthood

As teenagers, they are in the process of growing up into adulthood and they are going through several psychological processes which are beyond their control. So as adults around them, we are expected to assist them through this period of growth with their personality and well being, intact.

WHAT THE TEENAGERS ARE CONFRONTED WITH

As a result of anger, he has a strong belief that the parents are wicked and too strict on him for no just cause, hence his rebellious tendencies and wild reaction can be occasionally displayed.

As much as possible, parents and other adults around them should not allow a situation that could trigger off rebellion in them. It can have a devastating effect on their lives and thwart their destiny.

THEY WANT TO BE TREATED LIKE ADULTS AND RESPECTED LIKE YOUNG ADULTS THAT THEY ARE.

(a) **Adapting to a new image i.e. change in appearance:** it is a transitional stage from childhood to adulthood, so it is a period where the indications of puberty sets in. Biologically, the boys start growing hairs in their private parts, arms, armpit and face (beard) . The girls grow pubic hairs and start menstruating - psychologically - they seek for independence and tend to believe that they are more knowledgeable and wiser than their parents and other adults around them. They rather believe more in their mates or peers. They have the ability to think better at this stage, if they are well handled by the adults around them. Some of them think of romantic partners at this level, if they have not been well mentored since childhood by their parents and the adults around them to know that such thoughts should be waved off at this stage, until later in life. Remember that they will only agree with you if you have been a friend to them not just a parent or relation. If they have been brought up to love and fear God, they will be able to control their emotions better at this stage.

PHYSICALLY - At this level, they grow taller and in some cases, they increase in weight etc. They find it too difficult to cope with all the various developmental processes at the same time. So, for an teenager who have friendly parents who interact with him intimately, with whom he could discuss these all encompassing development, he will be able to cope easily without deviating from the norms. Otherwise his friends and peers who do not know better than him will be his mentors and counselors. It will result into the story of two blind men leading themselves on. It is obvious that they will both fall into a pit.

(b) <u>**It is also a time of mood-swing for them.**</u> In adapting to a new mental capacity, they analyze facts in a more matured and abstract way. They struggle with their body changes, peer pressure, self image and social issues as well as acting out their need for their parents to trust in them and let them be independent indeed.

(c) <u>**He faces the growing academic demands at school.**</u> He has more subjects to take in school. The various subjects are getting detailed and more intricate passing every session. He is expected to be able to cope adequately despite all odds. He must be able to grapple adequately with all the subjects at school successfully, knowing fully well that failure will result into being scolded by his parents and disgraced among his peers. He will want to tag on with his peers because failure results into being dropped off from a group of achievers to the group of "The No future Ambition" i.e (the NFA)/ He knows that they are very good at laughing at themselves, so he will avoid the disgrace by all means.

(d) Increased verbal ability and a wider scope of vocabulary is expected of him as he progresses in his academic endeavour from one level to another, as well as his involvement in social activities. He has to be able to express himself as he evolves as a leader e.g. every student in a senior class is expected to be able to lead and address those in the junior classes. He is also expected to be able to lead the younger ones in the family and in the church as well. So he is faced with the challenge of living up to expectation in this area of life, if he has enough confidence and exposure to do it without being criticized, he will master it faster.

(e) **He is expected to live an adult and responsible life style.** He has to be able to control his impulses and exhibit a matured behavior otherwise the parents and other adults around him will accuse him of being childish, even without any tutelage on the attainment of the teenage age. They will simply criticize him of behaving in a childish manner. In order to avoid such a ridicule, he must learn to comport himself in a responsible manner. It is a task, especially if he is not been encouraged and aided along this time, earlier.

(f) **They will have to learn to control their sexuality:** At this point of development, they will have to make a lot of important decisions in relation to their own sexual behavior. Regular counseling by parents and all the other well meaning adults around them will be of a great assistance to them at this level. Exposure to the Word of God is also a key factor that can help them surmount this period successfully and grow into a matured, disciplined and dependable adult.

(g) <u>Peer Pressure</u>: This can have a very strong effect on them at this stage of development. Parents should take time to have a heart to heart talk with them from time to time about how and why they must avoid having bad friends; how to identify a bad friend. Emphasize the repercaution of relating with a bad group, in his own interest.

The average human being is selfish. If the reason why they should avoid them is because of you or anyone else, they will ignore the advice. Let them know how and why it is in their own interest. The advice of a parent will easily be taken by them, if a friendly relationship has been developed earlier with them. They will believe that you love them, that is why you don't want them to miss the mark, but if they believe you are too strict, wicked and hostile to them, they will just listen out of courtesy, pretend in your presence and still misbehave in your absence but once you can win their friendship, love and confidence, they will try not to disappoint you, except if they mistakenly do it.

In such a situation, they will apologize and ensure that they prevent a reoccurrence, by so doing, they will become self disciplined. It will serve as a lesson of how to get themselves restrained from doing anything bad or wrong.

They don't ever attempt to please anybody who does not believe in them, except for the fear of being punished and all they will do is to pretend and never take the advice serious. They see it as a good way of punishing somebody whom they believe, hated them. When they misbehave before him and grossly disobedient, they intentionally want to stress such a parent.

It is difficult to get them conformed by a parent or any adult who is not a friend to them. They will rather relate with and imitate their peers, because they believe that they love them.

They are very good at ganging up against their parents or any adult who is against them, whether at home or in school. They support one another against the adults in any supposed case of intimidation. Parents should notice that they hardly speak ill of one another before adults but if any of them had done anything wrong, they will rather correct the person among themselves rather than report him to an adult or their parents. They hardly ridicule their peers before adults and parents. They can only resort to doing so if such a person shows some element of stubbornness or incorrigibility to them. They can be very co-operative whether positively or negatively.

However, it has been observed that, for teenagers who have very good moral foundation and upbringing, this transition period will not be marked with any calamity or gross misbehavior as I have mentioned. So, as parents let us "catch them young", so, start an adequate parenting from childhood so that it will swing swiftly into the teenage stage of life without any problem as the child grows into adulthood as a teenager. The mistake many parents make is that once the child becomes a teenager, they will stop parenting him, because they believe that he is old enough to take care of himself at that point. Although this is quite right to some extent, but they still need our assistance, not as a baby or a young child to be coached but now, as an intimate friend to be mentored and guided. We have passed that way before, so we are to lead them through it, amicably in a friendly manner so that they can open up to us, without which we will not be able to help them and when there is any problem, we will have to face it together. Why not ensure then that there is no problem at all.

Chapter ⑦
Further Strategies
for the
Parenting
Of
Teenagers

FURTHER STRATEGIES FOR THE PARENTING OF TEENAGERS

In addition to the earlier mentioned tips about parenting of your teenage child, the following steps are also recommended.

1. Always listen to them carefully before talking. Don't do all the talking because you believe that you know it all. They can be very intelligent if you allow them to talk.If you just conclude that he has nothing meaningful to say, he might not get matured fast enough, you will not know why he took the step you might be rebuking him for. It is also a sign of down-playing his intelligence and they hate that, even if they cannot tell you.

2. Show a lot of interest in his/her world, so that he can open up to you and grow up as a confident young man or lady.It will also enable you to be able to counsel and mentor him.

3. Whenever you are having a discussion with him, make sure you take note of what he is saying, his tone of voice, facial appearance and body language in order to be able to understand specifically what he is trying to express.

4. Never shout on him or talk to him angrily. He will just switch off and not listen to you again, he might just stand before you as a matter of courtesy and he will not turn a new leaf. If he knows that you are very strict, he will only pretend that he is obedient and grossly misbehave in your absence, but if you talk to him as you would address your age mate who had done a wrong thing, he will feel remorseful and apologize. He will henceforth avoid committing the same mistake again.

5. Avoid uttering negative comments and pronouncement on your child because he has done something wrong. All your statements over him, whether good or bad will

happen to him, because as a parent, you are an authority figure in the life of your child. When God gives a man any responsibility, he usually adds authority to it for effectiveness. God Himself was the one who created us and the children belong to Him, but He has assigned them to various families for administrative purposes. Hence, we were all in different families before under our various parents.

One by one, we left our respective families to start off our individual families. So, as parents, we are caretakers of the children. One day, we will give an account to God of how well we have cared and nurtured the children he sent to our respective families for grooming.

So, instead of saying negative things to your child when he errs, turn it into a positive statement. It will still reflect whatever you have in mind after all. Otherwise, it will have a devastating effect on the destiny of the child.

6. Endeavour to always have a one-on-one, heart-to-heart talk with him on an indepth level, not only about what he is doing presently or about his movements etc but also about his doubts, fears, aspirations, confusion, wishes and dissatisfaction. Let him be able to tell you anything and ask you any question without any reservation - be close to him enough to get to that level.

7. Don't only rebuke him for any fault you find in him but rather also acknowledge his merits and qualities with clear words of appreciation. This will enable him to believe that you love him and that you are indeed his parents and you are not only hostile always. They don't struggle to please anybody whom they have perceived as someone who hates them.

8. Avoid expression that can stop you from communicating with him. Once he believes that you are always picking on him, he will start avoiding your presence. This will hinder you from parenting him adequately and it can be disastrous to his life and destiny. They hate to be embarrassed by their parents or any adult around them, especially in the presence of others.

9. Don't insist on your own ideas. Let him take some guided decision too as an adult-in-training. Make your points clear and don't impose your view on him except you think it is very important that you do so, but don't be surprised that he can disobey you blatantly in some instances. If you don't impose it on him and you are friendly enough with him, he will still think about it and take your advice.

10. Never hesitate to apologize to him whenever necessary. If you believe that you offended him, he will appreciate your apology, emulate your humility, he will also love and respect you more for it.

11. Always keep his secrets secret. Otherwise, if he realizes that you have been telling others whatever he has been telling you in secret, he will shut off completely from you, no matter how much pressure he is undergoing on any issue. It will therefore become very difficult for you to help him out of any agonizing situation.

12. **<u>Don't ever compare him to any other child or individual.</u>** A teenage child gets thrown off balance. If this is done. He will simply write himself off and believe that he cannot amount to anything especially as adjudged by a major authority figure in his life; i.e. the father or the mother. Appreciate that every child is unique, even the identical twins have some unique features that make one

different from the other. Every creature of God has something to offer to the world. Find out what makes each child unique and assist him in developing it to the maximum. No creature of God can be completely useless.

13. **Lead him by example:** Showcase to him through your way of life what you expect him to do that will be approved by you. Leading by example is the best form of leadership. Children may not listen to the adults around them but they have never failed to imitate them.

14. **Believe in him and let him know it.** Don't ever give up on any child. If a parent gives up on a child, it can be very devastating.

15. **Let there be no favouritism.** Only bad parents have favourites among their children and declare it to others. Make sure that you treat your children equally no matter the situation. Each child has a unique selling point. Discover it and love him for it as you assist him in developing the other positive traits. Don't keep criticizing him and declaring him as redundant and bad. He will lose confidence in himself and may never be able to behave better.

16. **Let him acquire some vocational skills in addition to his academic certificates. so that he could enjoy a multiple streams of income as an adult.** His earnings will not just be from one source. Whenever my children were on holidays, when they were in the secondary school and immediately after their final exams at the end of their secondary school education, they went in for Vocational training of different kinds ranging from dressmaking, catering, computer (soft/hardware), barbing and horticulture. Today in addition to their academic qualifications they also have enterprises based

on the vocational training they had. The beauty of it is that once he has the knowledge and the money to establish, he will set up various businesses and get experts in the various fields to mann it for him while he assumes a supervisory role on about three or four businesses. His academic qualification will fend him some money too.

Without the vocational skill acquisition, he will only depend on his certificate which can only fetch one source of income. God has given us our hands to make money not only to hold pens to write and always waiting for the next salary which comes in every 30 days.

17. Know his friends and discourage him against moving with bad ones in his own interest.

18. **Make sure you are close to him enough to be able to know his movements so that he does not mistakenly run into trouble.** It is necessary for you to let him know that you understand and love him, then he will be honest with you absolutely, without hiding anything from you.

19. Seek to be his accountability partner. By so doing, he will not want to find himself in any situation that is shady.

Chapter 8

Good *Relationship* with **GOD** is Non-negotiable

Good Relationship With God

1. Let them form the habit of memorizing the scriptures. It will be stored in their sub-conscious and surge into their memory whenever they are to be corrected or commended. It is like a raw material which will be used by the Holy Spirit to direct them when nobody else will be there. I worked as a Principal and later an Educational Administrator in some secondary schools where this was practiced. The students memorized a verse of the Scriptures every week, compulsorily. It means that in a term they would have memorized twelve or thirteen verses of the Scriptures depending on the number of weeks in that term. At the end of the term the students were made to write an exam on it where they would be asked to quote all the verses memorized that term and explain two of them in details. The pass mark was 70%. The test was referred to as the ethics test. If any Prefect or Class Captain scored below 70%, he or she was debadged and removed as a Prefect or Class Captain immediately because the blind cannot lead the sighted person, they will both fall into a pit.

   A boy, who was an ex-student, then attending a private University came to see me in my office one morning to relate his experience to me. He was in his third year then. He told me that, on Campus whenever he wanted to do anything wrong, the verse of the Scriptures that could hinder him from doing it would just surge into his memory in such a way as if it was an individual insisting that he must not do it, he would obey immediately and gradually he was different from the other students. He was very well behaved and found dependable by his Lecturer and mates. He said that he was made a class governor in no time.

   No wonder the Psalmist said "Thy Word O God have I hid in my heart, so that I will not sin against you."

2. When my children were teenagers, I did the same thing for them. All of us together will decide on the verses of the Scriptures to be memorized every month. The recitation test would usually come up at the end of every month, before they would collect their pocket money. Only those who could recite the four verses of the Scriptures for the month without any mistake were given the pocket money.

   Also once a week, we held a family Bible study that would last for one and half hours in the evening, it was led by the children one after the other on weekly basis. As parents, we initially guided them on the preparation and encouraged them after by commending them on the very good delivery of the message. As time went on they became expert preachers right from home. When they entered the University, they were all pastors on their various campuses and now they are all workers in the Church. The foundation of that was laid at home by the parents, then the Holy Spirit took over.

   It is not enough to just take them to Church, it is important that you lay the foundation of a meaningful spiritual life for them at this level. Please note that if they don't see you as a friend, they will not see any reason why they must do whatever you direct them to do. If you force them, they will just be pretending to follow you.

3. As parents, one day we will be at home when they will travel out of the country and be on their own. Later they will start working and move out of the house to start their own families after marriage, the parents will no longer be there

4. Parents are expected to get their children - especially those young adults prepared for a life of their own shortly after attaining the teenage age, by ensuring that

they have an intimate relationship with God. They should know who God really is and how to relate with him, genuinely to settle whatever problem they encounter. We are to teach them from childhood how to have their morning devotion, read their Bibles and pray every day as they grow up. At the teenage stage, they should be leading the daily family devotion; they should be rendering one service or the other in the vine yard of God as a way of preparing them for their future roles in the Kingdom of God. We are all saved to serve.

(iii) As parents, we are to assist them in their spiritual growth too as we do in their biological, social, psychological and academic growth. In fact growing spiritually in an adequate dimension is the climax of the matter. So, it must not be left out.

Such a life will be directed and led by the Holy Spirit Himself and the destiny of the child will be easily actualized without any stress on the parents. It simply makes it easier. This is the key.

Chapter ⑨
How to **Draw** the line as a **Parent**

It is very important for parents to ensure that despite the lofty handling of the teenage child, they should still know their limits and realize that their parents must be respected and obeyed.

The following steps should be taken for precaution:

1. Decide on what must not be compromised e.g. Don't compromise your parenting duties, it is divine; hence no going back on ensuring that the child turns out to be a responsible and acceptable member of any nation, society or community wherever he finds himself now, always and forever.

2. Have a family guiding principle which must be imbibed by every member of the family as a core value, which will not be compromised for any reason.

   When we were growing up as children in my family, I remember that my father was always telling us repeatedly that "Good name is better than riches." He kept on storing this statement in our subconscious mind and today, it has helped us to be men and women of integrity. My mother on the other hand kept on telling us that once you are reminded before you carry out any legitimate assignment, it is a clear indication of irresponsibility. I knew the meaning of the word "irresponsibility" since I was 4 years old.

   As parents, we must manage our children the right way so that they do not tarnish the reputation of the family by soiling our hard earned names and reputation.

3. Draw a list of items that you cannot compromise with your teenage children in a friendly atmosphere. Let them be the ones to make all the suggestions, because they

know fully well what mum and dad can never allow them to do. Tell them to add the necessary sanctions to the rules as you all do it together and allow them to take the lead, since it is meant for them. Agree on the terms together. It is like drawing up a family constitution and you are all delegates to the conference. It will be ratified by the president and vice-president of the family i.e. mum and dad.

They will all keep to it whole heartedly. If they violate any of such rules drawn up by themselves, it will be an error and they will apologize immediately and prevent a reoccurrence. This will enable them know what they can be allowed to do and what they must not do, in their own interest.

4. If anyone violates any of the rules, the sanction must be applied without any sentiment. They will obey willingly and grow up to be highly responsible adults.

5. Give them regular informal motivational talks to ensure that they are well mentored and know how to avoid being sanctioned. It is wrong to have a set of rules for children and not teach them how to obey the rules and avoid the punishment. Whatever an individual does repeatedly and consistently unabated will become a habit. They will develop a habit of discipline and grow up to be ladies and gentlemen of integrity.

Chapter 10

Self Esteem
and how it
Affects
Teenagers

DEFINITION: Self-esteem is a person's opinion of himself. High self-esteem is a good opinion of yourself and low self esteem is a bad opinion of yourself. We all have a mental picture of who we are, how we look, what we are good at and what our weaknesses are. This picture is developed over time.

It started from when we were young. So, the term self-image is used in referring to a person's mental picture of himself. It is mainly based on our interaction with other people and our life experiences in general. Self-esteem is all about how you feel valued, loved, accepted and thought well of, by others and how much you value, love and accept yourself. People with healthy self esteem feel happy about themselves. They appreciate their own worth, take pride in their abilities, skills and accomplishments; while on the other hand, people with low self esteem feel that no one likes them, accepts them or believes that they can succeed in anything e.g. their studies.

Self esteem can be improved upon. A child should not be allowed to believe that he was being punished or scolded because he was not loved. This should be carefully taken care of by his parents and all other adults as they punish him whenever necessary.

UNHEALTHY SELF-ESTEEM

An unhealthy self-esteem in a child can be as a result of how he is being treated by others and how he sees himself. This can have a great impact on the self-esteem of the individual.

1. Parents and other authority figures influence the ideas we develop about ourselves, especially the children we handle. As parents and care-givers, etc. if we spend more time criticizing a child than praising him. It can affect the self-esteem of the child, especially because as

teenagers, they are still in the process of forming their own values and beliefs aboutthemselves.

If he is often criticized, he will develop an "inner voice" critic, modeled after the voice of his most ardent critic. This voice criticizes him whenever he is attempting to do anything positive or negative, to the point where he gives up on life and sees himself as a failure.

2. The term self-esteem comes from a Greek word meaning "reverence for self." The "self" pertains to values, beliefs and attitudes that we hold about ourselves. The word "esteem" describes the value and worth that is given to oneself. Self esteem is indeed an acceptance of ourselves for who and what we are at any given time in our lives.

Self esteem has two sources;

(a) Internal source (one's own accomplishment)
(b) External source (affirmations and comments from others).

WHY IS SELF ESTEEM IMPORTANT IN OUR INTERACTION AS PARENTS WITH OUR TEENAGE CHILDREN?

How we feel about ourselves can influence how we live our lives. Children with high self esteem relate better with others. They believe they can accomplish goals and solve problems. They are result oriented and focused. Having a good self esteem allows him to accept himself and live life to the fullest, while it is the opposite for those with low self-esteem. Self- esteem plays a vital role in almost everything we do. People with high self-esteem do better in school, find it easier to make friends, feel happier and find it easy to deal with mistakes.

As parents, we are to preserve the self-esteem of our teenage children so that they can end up being great achievers who will impact their generation.

UNHEALTHY SELF-ESTEEM COULD DEVELOP AS A RESULT OF ONE OR MORE OF THE FOLLOWING

To arrive at the point where an unhealthy self-esteem will set in:

a. The child re-evaluates his past experiences and influences

b. Information through uncomplimentary remarks about himself through his parents, friends and others. All these put together affect his self-esteem.

c. **APPEARANCE:**
    Teenagers are usually conscious of their appearance. They worry about their hair, complexion, clothes and their weight. Any criticism of their appearance will affect their self-esteem.

d. **PERFORMANCE:**
    A teenager's performance is as a result of an estimate of himself or herself, formed by how others and himself view his or her developing abilities, skills and intelligence e.g. he passes comment like "I am not good at Maths", "I cant do anything right." etc such experiences and beliefs about himself can contribute to a low self-esteem.

e. **STATUS**
    The social structure within which a growing child lives and functions can affect the child's self-esteem especially if he is conscious of it. In most cases, teenagers and their peers base their status on who they like, who likes them, whether they are popular or not, what kind of cars their parents have, what their parents do and how rich they are, where they live etc. All these add up together to create the self- concept the teenage child holds of himself.

f. **UNREALISTIC EXPECTATIONS:**
This can also affect a person's self-esteem. People have an image of who they want to be or who they think they should be. People who see themselves as having the qualities they admire usually have high esteem and people who don't see themselves as having the qualities they admire may develop a low self esteem.

g. **ABUSE:**
Research had shown that there is a high correlation between child abuse and low self esteem. This is not limited to sexual abuse or physical abuse. Emotional maltreatment at school such as sarcastic remarks from teachers, parents and other adults with whom they interact or unrefined disciplinary actions that could embarrass children in front of their peers is a form of abuse and it could lead to low self esteem, of the children concerned. Several mental health experts have confirmed that tactics such as "name calling," ridicule or sarcasm can rob a child of his self esteem.

h. **PARENTAL REJECTION**
Parental rejection of the child for any reason can lead to a low self esteem and eventual depression on the part of the child. It has been discovered that the children who were raised in a family environment of excessive parental criticism, belittling, ridiculing, neglect, lack of attention and where there is no parental love, care and concern are likely to struggle with the task of re-evaluating themselves and their places in the world. Many of them psychologically believe that they are non-entities and never-do-well who cannot succeed in life.

On the other hand, an over-protective teenage child might develop a sense of incompetence to take care of himself and this could result into a low self-esteem.

i. **FAULTYTHINKING:**
This is one of the manifestations of a low self-esteem. Such children who had been made to believe that they must get everything right by all means grow up to become slaves to perfection. Once they cannot meet the high standard set by their parents, teachers, peers or themselves on any issue, they develop a feeling of inferiority because they have based their self-worth on the ability to accomplish a goal. It is therefore better for a child to compete against himself. His rate of improvement is better measured against his previous performance, so that he could be praised and feel psychologically elated, even when a little success is attained. This could spur him to action, thereby achieving a greater feat, rather than struggling to get to the level of others in one day.

This can be frustrating and demoralizing to a child who is just coming up.

INDICATIONS OF UNHEALTHY SELF-ESTEEM

1. Pessimistic outlook to life
2. Lack of confidence in social issues and skills
3. Always too sensitive to the opinions of others
4. Too conscious about other people's opinion of his appearance, performance or status
5. A sense of masculinity or feminity felt only through sexual conquests.
6. The belief that God is unhappy with him or God is angry with him
7. A striving to become somebody or something in order to impress other people.

8. A habit of mentally rehearsing past conversations or situations, wondering what the other person meant
9. A critical and judgemental view of others
10. Defensiveness in behavior and conversation
11. Always having a feeling of been flattered whenever he is being praised.
12. Lack of confidence in himself
13. Fearofbeingalone
14. Dependence on material possession for security
15. The habit ofreferring to himself by using negative label
16. Anticipation or worry that the worst will happen
17. Following the crowd and avoiding independent behavior
18. Perfectionist behavior as regards details
19. Interpretation of their world as hostile and over- powering
20. A shifting of responsibilities to others for unwanted or n negative situations and feelings.
21. An excessively sensitive conscience
22. Relating only to people who are below the individual academically, socially or chronologically.

PARENTAL INVOLVEMENT THAT CAN BUILD UP A CHILD'S SELF ESTEEM

(a) If parents have a lot of positive and friendly interaction with their children, his self esteem will be higher.

(b) Unconditional positive acceptance of the child by his parents.

(c) Expectations of boundaries that are clear and firm without being authoritarian help the child to ascertain easily what behaviours are acceptable and the ones that must beavoided.

(d) Respect for our children as parents, coupled with a mixture of democratic and authoritative parenting style will have the most positive effect on the child's self-esteem.

(e) Parents' consistency in the method of handling a child enables the child to be able to know exactly the values he is expected to imbibe, cherish and maintain. It also reinforces the values of the child to the parents as it enhances his self esteem.

(f) If the children are empowered to be able to do some things on their own, take some decisions based on accepted norms and values of the family, they will become confident and capable individuals who believe in their abilities to attain greater heights.

(g) Children imitate what they see. Parents are to model the type of behaviours and attitudes they want their children to exhibit, right before them always. It should not be a matter of "Do as I say and not as I do."

Also, parents who face challenges of life could be exposing their children to examples of problem-solving strategies without knowing it (especially if the challenges were eventually surmounted successfully). This can enhance the children's self-esteem.

(h) Positive thinking - a positive perspective enables us to see the good things that life can offer us, not just the bad things it could provide . If this is imbibed by the child through tutelage by the parents by example, it will foster a positive self-esteem.

EXPERIENCES THAT CAN HAVE NEGATIVE EFFECTS ON THE CHILD'S SELF-ESTEEM

1. Repeated negative evaluation of others about him. If a child is repeatedly told that he is *II* stupid", too *II* slow" etc he is likely to believe such comments concerning himself.

2. Severe or repeated criticism reduces self-worth, self confidence and can be damaging to the child's self esteem e.g. if such a child is often said to be "below average" "a dollard" "not intelligent" "not brilliant." He will simply give up on himself. He will not aspire to improve.

3. Negative humour about a child can lead to a damaged self esteem.

4. After consistent mistakes, errors or failures, if the child is not encouraged by any adult or peer around, the self esteem of such a child can be affected and this can lead to a permanent indisciplined attitude to life, poor performance at school and an outright non-achievement in life . Once the child has been disciplined, after a misbehviour, he should be interacted with by the parents or the adult punishing him by a series of counseling talks in order to get him rehabilitated, otherwise his self esteem will be dented.

5. Embarrassment: An embarrassing situation could lead to lack of confidence and invariably lead to a low self esteem . An occurrence of this type should be avoid ed.

6. Comments about a child by the parents, teachers, peers and others around him determine the worth he places on himself. If the comments are positive, high self esteem will be developed; if the comments are negative, low self esteem will be the result.

STRATEGIES TO DEVELOPING HIGH SELF ESTEEM IN A CHILD BY THE PARENTS

(a) The children will watch and copy how their parents react to situations - successes and mistakes. Parents are to model positive responses and strategies for dealing with these experiences.

(b) Accept your children's behaviours and feelings. Sit them down to dialogue with them and correct them where necessary, instead of labeling the child as completely bad.

(c) Respect your teenage children and let them know that they are valued and respected as important members of the family. Parents must take a proactive interest in the affairs of their children.

(d) Listen to them whenever they have anything to tell you about themselves, then guide and counsel them as appropriate for an improved performance and behavior.

(e) Avoid having a favourite among your children. Treat all of them equally. Always spend quality time with them so that you can bond with them to get them impacted. The joy of a parent at this level of parenting is to get the child transformed from one commendable level to the other morally, spiritually, academically and also in every area of life.

(f) Parents are expected to promote competence and establish priorities that will engender high self esteem and self confidence in each child. He needs to be introduced to meaningful activities which will encourage him to achieve his potentials. Each child may have different potentials but it is equally crucial that their achievements are meaningful so as to increase their opinion of their capabilities. Self esteem will further be enhanced if children attain excellence performance in skills which are useful and of interest to them.

(g) Parents are to give specific feedbacks and promote realistic ideals in developing the self-esteem of their teenage children.

It is important for us to explicitly teach our children how to set realistic expectations for themselves. This can be done by giving feedbacks which will outline what they have achieved. We need to let children know that it is possible to make some mistakes in a learning process but it must be corrected and never to be repeated again. They will need our assistance as parents in accepting and recognizing feedbacks. It is always necessary for us to compensate a positive feedback for a repeated performance.

(h) Parents, teachers and all other adults parenting teenagers should have well structured limits and goals that could enable the children to compete with themselves and measure their level of improvement in behavior or academics as the case may be. This will enable them have a basis for evaluating their present performance and comparing it with the previous ones. This will enhance their self esteem.

PARENTS SHOULD GIVE A TEENAGE CHILD WITH A LOW SELF ESTEEM THE FOLLOWING ADVICE.

1. Don't always try to please others in an attempt for you to do the right thing, rather ensure that whether anybody sees you or not, you do only the right things, especially as God sees us anywhere we may be and He is the One we should first aspire to please at all times.
2. Start with small things, (activities and exercises) in order to gain confidence.
3. Avoid those who can influence you negatively. Don't compare yourself to others. Just be the best you can.
4. Face your fears and learn from your failures; let him know that when something does not go the way we expect, there is something to be learnt from it, which can be applied next time, if the person is in a similar position.
5. He should not think negatively about himself.
6. He should improve on his self confidence by doing things that he can accomplish, since accomplishment is the major ingredients in gaining self-confidence.
7. Do something to impress yourself e.g. he could learn a simple task to improve his ability to accomplish feats. This will improve his self-confidence, accomplishment and raise his self confidence.
8. Don't worry about being perfect. Just make sure that you achieve your goals.
9. Learn to appreciate yourself.
10. Commend and reward yourself when you succeed.

A lot depends on us as parents, guardians, care givers, teachers and all the other adults charged with the God given responsibility of nurturing, mentoring and raising our teenage children adequately to be able to fulfill the purpose of their existence and be best among their contemporaries wherever they find themselves all over the world. This is the desire of God for their lives and God is counting on us to perform diligently the part in the creative process we are scheduled by God to accomplish while he executes the rest. However, although God can do all things but He expects us to take the first step especially the bit He is sure we can carry out, then He will surprise us. A high self esteem is desired for the teenager to be a high achiever and your support is non-negotiable in this venture, for the desired excellence.

Chapter 11
The Uniqueness
Teenage
Children

The supremacy of God our creator should be recognized in the fact that no two individuals are exactly alike in everything, even identical twin are not totally similar in all things. It has been ascertained that no two human beings have the same finger prints. As parents we must take this truth of life into consideration as we relate with our children in general, especially in their teenage years. Once you compare one person to the other in their presence or to their knowledge, the one you have acknowledged to be inferior will get totally demoralized and write himself off as useless. So, avoid it completely.

Every individual is unique and specially designed for the purpose for which God has created him and sent him into the world to accomplish.

Always check for their strong points and assist them in developing it. Get them encouraged and let each child feel special, because they are all indeed special and unique.

As parents and all other adults positioned around them for grooming, we are to assist them in over-coming any weakness noticed in them due to their personality type and assist them also in enhancing their strength with regards to their behavior, academic work and activities.

FIND ENUMERATED HERE, VARIOUS PERSONALITY TYPES; THE STRENGTH AND WEAKNESSES OF EACH

Once you are aware of the personality type of your child, you will know what type of behavior to expect and be able to assist him in conforming to the required norms in any environment he finds himself now and in the future. A negative attitude can be worked on to be better.

WHAT IS PERSONALITY TYPE?

It is the various aspects of a person's character that makes the individual different from others.

PERSONALITY TYPES

Psychologists have found out that human beings can be grouped into four basic personality types, namely:

(a) Sanguine
(b) Choleric   EXTROVERT
(c) Melancholy
(d) Phlegmatic   INTROVERT

Expected Traits of a Sanguine Strength

- ❖ He is a warm, buoyant, lively and jolly person
- ❖ He is easily moved to tears
- ❖ He loves to please others
- ❖ He is outspoken and good at story telling
- ❖ He is comfortable around people and he doesn't like to be alone
- ❖ He never lacks friends
- ❖ He is compassionate
- ❖ His lovable disposition makes people to overlook his weaknesses.

Weakness

- He has a weak will and lacks self discipline
- He could pretend. He could also be deceitful, dishonest and undependable
- Restless and disorganized
- Prone to exaggerate
- Unstable
- Egoistical
- Noisy
- Talkative
- He is easily distracted

Expected Traits of a Choleric

- Strongwilled
- Self sufficient and independent
- Decisive and opinionated
- Make decisions for himself and other people
- Possession of endless ideas
- The environment does not stimulate him, he stimulates the environment
- He takes a firm stand on issues not minding what people think.
- He welcomes challenges and criticism.
- His dogged determination makes him succeed where others have failed.
- Active and energetic
- Not frightened by adversities but they rather strengthen him.

Weaknesses

- He is not emotional, he does not sympathize easily with others
- He is often embarrassed by tears
- He is extremely hostile
- He gets angry easily
- He has little appreciation for art and music
- He is sarcastic and cruel
- He is impatient
- He can be unforgiving

Expected Traits of a Melancholy Strength

- He is analytical, self sacrificing, gifted and a perfectionist
- Has appreciation for music and fine art
- Extremely loyal to the few friends he has
- Highly gifted
- Very neat and well co-ordinated
- Industrious
- Highly dependable
- Aesthetic and creative
- Highly sensitive

Weaknesses

- Wears his feelings on his sleeves (moody)
- Does not make friends easily
- He says very little in public and when he does, for days afterwards he condemns himself for imagined mistakes
- Easily offended
- Pessimistic
- Critical and picky
- Suspicious and revengeful
- Self centered
- Lacks self confidence
- He desires to be loved by others and finds it difficult to express his feelings.

Expected Traits of a Phlegmatic Strength

- Calm and easy going but humorous
- Avoid confrontations
- He could be orderly
- Never agitated, no matter the circumstances around him
- He is highly consistent
- Has a positive approach to life
- Polite and diplomatic
- When aroused to action, he is capable and efficient and his ability becomes apparent.
- When a leadership position is forced on him, he proves to be a very capable leader
- He acts as a natural peace-maker

Weakness

- Subjectto procrastination
- Apparent lack of drive and ambition
- Passive and unmotivated
- Selfish, self indulgent and unconcerned about the needs of others
- He is a miser
- Unsure and self protective
- He is stubborn
- He is slow and lazy
- Fearful and filled with worry
- He is reluctant to get involved in any other activity beyond his daily routine
- He never volunteers for leadership on his own.

Please Note:

It will be very rare or impossible to find somebody with only one personality type. Everyone has at least a combination of two or three; but there is usually a dominant one that can be more visibly noticed in the character of each individual.

Chapter ⑫

Personality Types of our Children
(Pre-Teens/Early Teens)
and
Academic Work

PERSONALITY TYPES OF OUR CHILDREN (PRE-TEENS/EARLY TEENS)

This topic is not related to the teenage children in the Upper Secondary School to the University level. It is mainly relevant to our children in the Primary Schools up to the last class of the Junior Secondary School.

At the Senior Secondary School level, the senior teenage age group, a child who has been adequately handled by the parents is expected to have been matured enough to the extent of being committed to his studies for an excellent performance, on his own.

Sanguine Students and their Academic Work

Traits displayed in class:

1. **They are easily distracted during lessons,** thereby preventing learning from taking place, if not curbed.
2. **Talkative:** This could be done during lesson or in the absence of a teacher in class. The effect of this is that he disturbs in class, distracts attention and encourages others to make noise too.
3. **Restless:** During lessons, he moves around the class, taking what belongs to other students, causing commotion and uproar. If not curbed, he disturbs the peace of the entire class.
4. **He is disorganized:** His books, could be tattered and unkempt; his uniform will always be very untidy; buttons left undone, dirty socks etc. His class work and assignments are usually left uncompleted, undone or wrongly done. He might not be able to provide some of his books, or submit most of his assignments at the expected time for his teacher to mark. He will not do his correction most of the time. Most of his textbooks would have been missing, with relevant pages off.

5. **Exaggeration:** He exaggerates a lot. He will tell a long story about why his class work is uncompleted and why he failed to do his assignment. He tells several exaggerated stories to cover up in order to avoid being punished.

6. **Instability as regards his performance.** If he is well monitored consistently by his parents, who understand him and who are there for him to ensure that his performance will improve. Once there is a break, his performance might drop. So, he has to be continuously monitored to do his work until he gets to a point where he would have started scoring very high marks, then he will likely go on gradually to the top and maintain it at the top with your support, grooming and monitoring, until he can stand on his own eventually.

The information about his personality type will get you, as his parents armed enough to assist him in overcoming his weaknesses and enable him to improve on his attitude from time to time. He will be eager to maintain high marks, from then on, he will likely sit up to a very serious hard work on his own, with little or no supervision. The moment he improves slightly e.g. from scoring 30%, and moving on to score 40% he should be praised and compensated with a prize, if that is done, he will aspire to do more and this will lure him into more commitment to his academic work.

He will keep improving as you encourage him. Don't expect him to start shooting up suddenly from 40% to 80%. It is possible, but it is likely to be gradual.

THE CHOLERIC AND ACADEMIC WORK

Traits Displayed in Class:

1. Impatient
They can be impatient with everything hence, they miss out important facts during lessons.

2. Anger
They get angry when things are not done the way they like as a result of which they could decide not to listen to the teacher again in class out of anger. He can walk out on the teacher, if he is allowed.

3. Hostility
He could be hostile to the teacher and other students in class. He could pass a comment that destabilizes everybody in class or put up a silent verbal response that can disrupt the on-going smooth sailing class activities.

4. Domineering
He dominates over all other students in class in order to display his ability. The effect of this is that other students will become intimidated.

5. Over Confidence
He demonstrates that he knows everything. This could affect his performance negatively as he might not want to settle down to learn, believing that he knows everything already. He might even spend his time in learning the wrong thing due to over confidence.

Melancholy Student and Academic Work

Traits displayed in class:

1. **Moody:** He could be moody and become withdrawn from all activities.

2. **Unfriendly:** He desires to be loved by others. If other students or pupils decide not to relate with him for any reason, his academic work will be affected because, he will feel dejected and this will affect the learning process.

3. **Easily offended and sensitive:** He gets offended and he is highly sensitive to any comment made about him. He has the tendency of thinking about such comments continuously until it starts affecting the learning process, because he will eventually get distracted, loses focus, becomes absent minded in class, by so doing. Once this is observed by his parents, they should quickly counsel him against it, so that he can stop doing so.

4. **Self Centered:** He prefers keeping things to himself instead of sharing it with others. If the class activity on hand requires co-operation, he will not be able to cope and this will affect his performance in such a task.

5. **Lacks Self Confidence:** He is afraid to do certain things successfully. This could lead to lack of participation in class discussion and he might not want to answer questions in class for fear of getting the answer wrong.

The Phlegmatic and Academic Work

Traits displayed in class:

1. **Procrastination:** He procrastinates about everything. The effect of this on his school work is that he does not study on a regular and consistent basis. He does not do his assignments on time and he will usually submit them late, after the deadline given by the teacher.

2. **He is passive and unmotivated:** This results into his being slow at doing things in general, hence he hardly completes his notes and class work. He could slow down the work of other members of his class, where the teacher expects the whole class to move on at about the same pace e.g. copying of notes in class or during a class activity that requires a teamwork.

3. **He lacks internal drive:** He is usually complacent and satisfied with the way he is. He lacks ambition. This can affect his academic work since he is not bothered about whether he scores a high mark or not, in a home work, test or examination.

4. **Unconcerned:** Heisneverbotheredaboutanything.This is capable of affecting his performance in his class work, especially as he will not participate in class.

5. **Fearful:** He is always afraid of getting involved in his school work and activities. He believes that he cannot cope. So, he decides to be withdrawn from class activities and discussions.

6. **Does not want a change of daily routine:** He prefers a consistent daily routine without any change. If there is any change in routine in the teaching and learning process, he

gets off balance e.g. transfer from one school to another or change in the system of teaching by a teacher will get him destabilized. So, as his parent or teacher, you have to allay his fears and get him reassured of success.

As parents, in order to assist them in settling down appropriately to their studies and overcome the challenges observed in any of the personality types enumerated in this chapter, we must be there for the child by playing the role of a Counsellor to him regularly instead of expecting him to behave, respond and perform like the others, on his own.

Chapter 13

Counselling your Children Effectively – The Teenagers and the Younger Ones

In order to ensure that the children overcome the challenges posed by their respective personality types, as I have enumerated in the last chapter, parents must counsel them regularly until they are able to conform and overcome almost all the weaknesses, if not all and grow up to be matured, intelligent and very responsible adults.

SOME TIPS THAT COULD HELP YOU IN THE COUNSELLING PROCESS

a. Be a role model to them and be very friendly with them - show a genuine concern otherwise your counseling will not be effective and you will therefore not be able to help them out.

b. Counseling is more psychological than physical. The fact that the person you are counseling seem to be paying attention to you does not mean he is really listening. So, it is essential for you to be sure that he believes in you. This must be properly worked out and ascertained to be so, before you can make a success of the counseling spree, that is why, as parents we must be very good friends of our children, so that we can have the desired access into their lives for such a period when it will be required, otherwise the child will rather prefer to go on with the problem without any solution than listening to a parent whom he considers a tyrant, who hates him.

c. Teenagers have a world of their own that no adult can easily penetrate into if they do not willingly allow him in - whosoever the adult may be. They co-operate with one another to a large extent. They easily gang up.

d. If you are the bossy type who wants to prove that you are strict, they will get you frustrated. So, intersperse your strictness with friendliness. If you are only friendly but not strict at all, they will abuse it. If you are only strict but not friendly, they will wearyououtinfrustration.

Parents and adults around them are advised to be friendly with them and only get displeased with them whenever they misbehave. If it is done this way, they will avoid misbehaving and try to please you all the time, in order to continuously be your friend. However, once they notice that you can't be pleased, they will not waste their time trying to please such an adult, no matter who he is. This is why parents or adults around them, who are continuously strict find it more difficult to get them reformed, they will just start misbehaving more. Such children will simply become incorrigible.

e. As you take the step to counsel a teenager, if you have not been friendly with him, he will start suspecting that you simply want to oppress and intimidate him because of your position- father, mother, senior siblings, teachers etc. His reaction will be that he will simply get more hardened and hate the person more. He will damn all the consequences of his action. Friendship with your children should start from the cradle. Teenagers believe more in their peers and open up more to them. So, in some cases get his siblings who are teenagers to also talk to him in a friendly manner if he is misbehaving. They have a way of handling themselves.

f. Keep his secret, secret:
If he confides in you, don't tell anybody about it except with his permission.

COUNSELLING PROCEDURE:

1. Ask questions that could give you an insight into the discoveries you want to make about whatever you want to counsel him against.

2. Show an in depth level of concern for his plight and open his eyes and understanding to perceive it too.

3. When you are counseling him, nobody else must be there and he should not be distracted in anyway because it is a psychological process. It requires a complete attention before it can be effective.

4. Be very analytical to let him know the side effects of any of the negative behaviours you want to correct him about i.e. the repercaution. Let him know that it is in his own interest, if he does it the right way.

5. Let him know the advantages of doing it the right way as well, in his own interest.

6. The truth is that whatever negative character you discovered in the child that will need to be corrected, must have been noticed by him too, but he might not know how to get it corrected or normalized. So, you have to let him know what to do, to overcome his weakness or short-coming.

7. The principal thing in counseling is to get the counselee to be conscientized and feel sorry about his previous way of life about the matter before the counselee can be challenged enough to turn a new leaf immediately. It is essential for you to get to that point with him. So, you can't counsel an individual when any of you is in a hurry.

8. It is necessary for you to catalogue his good deeds before mentioning the bad ones. This will enable him open up to you and listen better.

9. Counseling is not a one off thing. It has to be continuous but the duration will be getting shorter as he complies. The frequency of your meeting with him will be getting reduced by the day, as he complies.

10. It is important to have a follow-up time with him just to know how far he has changed per time. Do this in a very friendly manner as someone who is concerned about his progress and welfare.

11. As he complies, even if it is gradual, start commending him for it and reward him with some prizes in order to encourage him to do more, this will enable him know that you are really interested in him.

    Parents believe that their children should know that as their parents, they are duty bound to love them but in some cases, they judge your love for them by the way you relate with them. If they conclude that you love their siblings more than them, for any reason best known to them, they will hate you for it and never believe in you too. They will be ready to kick against your orders behind you. They will always be prepared to rebel against such a parent in his absence and pretend to be well behaved in his presence in order to avoid the punishment you might want to mete out to them if you get to know that they are just pretending.

    This is not good enough, because at the end of the day, he will turn out to be a bad child helplessly, at a time when the parents too will feel sad and ashamed of it.So, let's do it right from the onset,for the benefit of all.

12. Apart from the academics, other characteristics that could be a danger sign to indicate that the child is in trouble and must be regularly counseled for improvement are the following reactions.

(a) Total withdrawal from everybody

(b) Extremely loud and troublesome

(c) Consistently low academic performance and attainment

(d) A boy who womanizes or a girl who is often in love with boys and men continuously.

(e) A boy or girl who likes partying

(f) A girl who likes dressing nude and indecently

(g) Always confrontational with adults

(h) Easily irritated and touchy

(i) Always absent minded

(j) Always isolating himself at home

(k) Always doing some secret things in the house and keeping it away from everybody else.

(l) Too secretive about himself and his personal affairs

(m) Very quarrelsome and abusive.

Please note that counseling a child is not only for reformation purposes. It is not only for when the child has done something wrong or misbehaves. As parents, it is a means of guiding our children through the path of life. We have passed through the streets, roads and junctions of life that they have never got to yet. We have experienced several things in life, some good, some bad. In some cases, some things did not happen to us directly, it was experienced by some other people around us, which had some disastrous consequences on them and which we don't want our children to experience, especially as they do not know the implications of their actions about these issues, hence counseling must be applied.

As parents, we are to spend quality time with them as we share these experiences by way of counseling them, so that they don't become victims of such negative experiences. They are expected to emulate the positive experiences you share with them and live up to expectation. The prayers of parents, teachers and other adults responsible for raising them in addition to regular counseling, will bring out the giant in them.

SOME TIPS THAT WILL GUIDE YOU IN GROUP COUNSELLING

Children can be counseled at home together in a situation where they are just to be guided. This should be on a regular basis. God has made you a guardian to them.

The following tips will be of assistance as you regularly play your counseling role in their lives, especially the teenage ones in order to guide them ahead, so that they don't slip off the slippery path of life as they journey on.

STEPS:

1. The topic should be relevant and purposeful
2. The atmosphere should be casual and cordial
3. Ensure that they get conscientized
4. State why the act is beneficial i.e. if the counseling is geared towards encouraging them to emulate a good deed.
5. If you intend to discourage them from a negative act, then, let them know the repercaution of towing that line of action, in their own interest.
6. Let them know in details what they have to do specifically either to avoid the bad acts or practice the good ones. They need to know how to go about it.

7. Repeat yourself always on issues you don't want them to forget so that it can be stored in their sub-conscious mind. Once it is stored there, it will usually surge up to their conscious mind as a reminder, whenever occasion demands for it. This is the essence of repetition by parents. If you do it often enough, whenever they are about to mistakenly carryout that wrong act, they will hear your voice in their minds as if you are just telling them and on the other hand, if they are to carry out the positive act, your voice will be heard in their minds as well by them and it will serve as a catalyst urging them to do it. So, repetition of your counseling tips to them is extremely good and very important. They will tell you that you always repeat what you have told them before, let them know that it is deliberate and it is in their own interest.

8. Share both direct and indirect experiences with them to buttress your point.

9. Demonstrate a lot of interest and concern for their future as you counsel them.

10. Always lay emphasis on the fact that you are concerned about their future and success in life - so everything you are telling them is all about putting their feet on the right path of life as one who had passed through that way before.

Also emphasize that your concern is to warn them against any danger that could be ahead and let them know the right precautions to take, so that they do not lower their guards, because even though experience is the best teacher, the school fees in his school is very expensive to pay and many things would have been irreparably destroyed before admission into that imaginable school. So, let them know that it is better to learn from the experiences of other people than to experience anything bad themselves. It is therefore better to be the subject matter of a good experience than a bad one.

Teenagers don't like repetition; they see it as a waste of their precious time. This is why you must let them know jokenly that your lesson with them can't be complete without repetition. Once you let them know the reason why you are doing whatever you do with them and they understand the reason why it has to be so in their own interest, they will no longer question it. They will fully co-operate with you and you will easily make a success of it.

As parents of teenage children, you must be a very good counselor to make a success of your parenting duty. It cannot be compromised if they have to be successfully parented. It is a divine duty and must be diligently carried out.

Chapter 14

The Teenage Children *from* Single Parent Homes *and how to* Raise Them

Definition of a Single Parent Home:

Many incidents can lead to a home being referred to as a single parent home. It simply means that a home where one parent is the only one available out of the two parents, for the parenting of the children in the family. It is compulsory for such a parent to lead by example, for an effective parenting.

It is very important for you to remember, as I have mentioned earlier on, that for the teenage child to believe in you and take you serious as his parents, teachers and other adults around them, you must BE A ROLE MODEL TO THEM. They have passed the stage of just obeying whatever you tell them to do, even if you act contrary. They are now at the point of "DO AS I DO AND NOT AS I SAY!!!

SINGLE PARENTHOOD CAN OCCUR AS A RESULT OF THE FOLLOWING:

(a) No marriage but has a child who is being catered for by either the father or mother alone

(b) Total abdication of parental responsibilities by a partner to the other alone

(c) Death of one of the parents

(d) Separation of parents due to disagreement

(e) Transfer of a parent to another nation or state and only one of the parents discharges the day to day parental duties of the home

(f) A prolonged absence of a parent from home for any reason

(g) Divorce - with one of the parents taking care of the children

(h) Desertation of a parent with the parental duties being discharged by only one of the parents available.

(i) In some cases, you have a couple living together in the same house, still claiming to be married, but due to negligence, irresponsibility or a type of job that could warrant a parent, going out in the morning and coming back at night on a daily basis and continuously, leaving all the decisions about the home and all other parental duties to the other parent alone. Such a home is also a single parent home. Raising of children is much more than paying their school fees and feeding them alone (although this is part of it). Come to think of it, people pay the school fees of those they are not related to and they feed them too, yet they cannot claim that they have parented such children. Just on the basis of that alone.

Parenting has to do with:

a. Giving birth to the children
b. Bringing them up.

However, some people found themselves in circumstances where they bring up the children they didn't give birth to themselves from infancy to adulthood. It is a divine duty. Although God has ordained that everything that is associated with raising of children and building a comfortable and conducive home for them should be borne by two people (The husband and Wife) and not just one person, but however due to some circumstances, sometimes beyond their control, some parents have found themselves as the only available parent on ground to take up this important responsibility. they are still expected to carry out the parental responsibilities as diligently as expected for the desired result of raising responsible, dependable and fulfilled young adults who will repay them for their labour when the time comes, instead of raising children, who will worsen their burden and increase their woes in old age.

So, there is need for a single parent to be more focused and self sacrificing in discharging the expected parental duties than when they were two. Some single parents in their anxiety to make ends meet, out of self pity, search for money any how to take care of the children; search for a partner to replace the unavailable one; they aspire to fall in love again and remarry hence they lose concentration and end up neglecting their children to their detriment. At the end of it all, these desires of theirs can be achieved, but the children would have been deserted without their knowledge. They would have started being parented by other people who can easily mislead them, sudden drop in academic performance could be suggestive of a problem the child was confronting and a careful investigation in terms of one on one discussion with such a child would need to be carried out, in order to redress the situation.

The rule was that, before they opened up to be counselled, I would have assured them of an absolute confidentiality, especially if it was suggested by them after our discussion, I would give them tips of solving the problems and they would be happy again.

Whenever there was any dire need to inform their parents, about the matter, (which we seldom did) the child in question must give his consent, otherwise, the matter would have to be settled between us, as long as he would be able to promise that things would change for the better on his own part, because he had a destiny to fulfill. In counseling them, we usually gave them some coping techniques for improvement. In most cases, the problem get solved without the knowledge of their parents.

Chapter 15

The Various Experiences of Teenagers
from
SINGLE PARENT HOMES IN SCHOOL

1. A boy, Sylvester Ayedowas in his third year in the Junior Secondary School. He was twelve years old then. The Mathematics teacher reported him to me that he was always avoiding classes. He would rather go to the Library and sit there doing nothing in particular. Some other teachers also reported him for not doing his assignments and submitting late even when he did. Having heard all these about Sylvester, I sensed that he had a problem that was outside his academics and the earlier it was resolved the better for him.

   I invited him for a heart to heart talk. This would not have been possible if I was not close to my students, just as a parent would do.

   He opened up to me about the concerns he had then that were affecting his focus, concentration and studies. He said that his mother was planning to marry the third husband and that he wouldn't like that because it would mean that he would be having a third sibling from another father, which would lead to a situation where the three children living with her would be of three different fathers and the boy felt that it would be indecent. He wondered how he could introduce his siblings to people in future, as children of the same mother bearing different surnames of three different fathers. He said that it was too odd and highly irresponsible of any woman to do that.

   I asked him why he had not discussed it with the mother. He said the mum was always angry with him whenever he raised the issue for discussion. He said he even thought of leaving the mother's house to go and live with his father, even though, he had never met him before, but someone gave him the description of the father and where he lived. According to him, he sneaked out of the house one day, when the mum was away to work (she was the Bank Manager of a first generation bank then) but on getting there, he was told that the Landlord of the house has just ejected him because he could not pay his rent but that he could be found in a beer parlour close to the house (which was situated in a low income and densely populated area of the state). He really went in search of him but he had to return home without seeing him, because on getting to the beer parlour, when he inquired about his dad, he was told that he could only be found there between 7:00pm and 10:00pm every day. Since it was not possible for him to leave home at such an odd time of the day, he had to go back home feeling disappointment, hence he lost his sense of focus and concentration absolutely. He said he kept on wondering why he had to be born into this world by such parents who were not bothered about the feelings of their children but just interested in their personal agenda.

He paused and started crying. I went to seat with him on the other side of my official table where he sat. He then passed a comment which struck me, that day. He said, "I don't lack anything at home. My school fees are always promptly paid by my mum, but that is not all about life. She is not considering the emotional pains, confusion and embarrassment I am going through because of the type of mess I have found myself in due to no fault of mine." He said further that whenever he was in class, his mind would always wander away especially because of this predicament, he would just be sitting down but not concentrating in anyway. I told him not to worsen the situation of things especially as he had no control over it.

I had to pacify him. I arranged a counseling routine with him, which coincided with break time (after his lunch and prep period, the last 20mins of it) I met him on a continuous basis for about two terms. I also developed a motherly relationship with him. He got settled down to his academics, after which he was given a free access to my office whenever he needed an advice or had any problem. I told him that he had to be the best that he could in his academics and behavior so as to attract the attention of the father (wherever he was) to start looking for his unique son when he becomes a National hero. I told him that this could start with being the best in all his external examinations. So, he must first settle down to a serious academic work that would enable him to be a force to be reckoned with in his academics.

He settled down to pursue these goals. I never discussed it with the mother and we got a consistent solution to the problem. If she had heard about it, she might believe that the boy was washing her dirty linen outside. The boy too would have stopped divulging any secret to me and would prefer to keep nursing it in his mind, which might have a devastating effect on his health and academics

2. A boy, Roland Ogbon was in the first year of a Junior Secondary School too at that time. He was the only son of the mum who was always coming to visit him in school and he was a boarder. Roland was always in the habit of coming to chat with me whenever he saw me moving around the school premises, especially whenever it was break time or a free period for him. I found out that his speech was always revolving around the absence of his father in the family and how dearly he loved him before he abandoned the family and left for somewhere unknown to his mother, since he was two years old.

When I observed that it was like a big challenge to his wholesome existence, judging by his utterance, I began to counsel him against such a feeling that was reflecting a low self esteem.

I gave him some coping techniques and was always praying with him.

I led him to Christ and told him that he had become a child of God, and that henceforth he should relate to God as his father because, as a matter of fact, God is the father of all fathers. I encouraged him to link up with the Holy Spirit in all situations as his guide, comforter and teacher because Jesus said that it was expedient that he should go to the father so that the comforter could come. He would teach us all things.

He got settled. I found out that he became more confident and full of life, I always repeated to him and others like him whom God in His Majesty brought my way as a teacher and principal, that since our fingers were not equal and our finger prints were not the same, as individuals, we could not have expected to have the same type of experiences in life.

So, whatever experience we have in life, we should remember that God had promised that He will never leave us nor forsake us hence, the part we needed to play was to hold tightly to our tenets of faith, flee from all appearances of evil, believe in Him and stand for Him wherever we found ourselves. I was always telling them to ensure that the constitution of the Kingdom of God i.e. the Bible was permanently their guide. In addition to these my usual charge to them was that they must ensure that they showcased academic excellence and discipline consistently, wherever they found themselves, so that they could end up being great achievers whom they had been destined to be, by God.

Roland became so settled that when he got to his final year in the school, he was the Assistant Head boy of the school. A post usually occupied by students who were disciplined and academically sound.

I was usually emphasizing to them that whatever challenge they had should be seen as a prayer point to be discussed with God for a solution, especially in situations where no human being can help us but as human beings we should not be worried over a problem we could not solve. We should rather solve the ones we could solve and cast the ones we could not solve on Jesus who willingly told us in the Bible that "Cast all our burdens upon Me because I care for you." I always repeated to them that "if you claim to cast it on Him and you are still disturbed about it, whatever it was, that will be a clear indication that you are still in full possession of those problems you can never solve, as a human being with limited power."

I kept on repeating this to all of them who had problems that were limiting their focus and concentration on their academics and had consequently started affecting their behaviors.

When Roland was in his final year in secondary school, in the second term of that session, he walked into my office one afternoon, after school on his way to the dormitory (he was a boarder) to give me the good news that the parents had just made up their differences and that the father had moved in with them. He then said that what he did, since I told him five years ago, when he was in his first year was to keep reminding God of his plight of not having a father who was living with the other members of the family in the same house, which was his utmost desire. In as much as he was not carrying the burden again, after casting it on Jesus, he became focused and kept on trusting in the Word of God which clearly emphasized that "Whatever you ask in prayer, believing, you will receive."

To this end, God answered Roland's prayer of belonging to an intact family and his academic work was not affected as he had one of the best results in all his final year external examinations and he immediately gained an admission into a high brow University in the UK for a course of his choice.

3. A boy Jenkins was in his third year in the junior secondary school. He was thirteen years old, then. Some teachers came to tell me that he was always absent minded in class. I immediately knew that he had a psychological problem which had started affecting his focus and concentration in class.

At that time, as the Principal of the school, I was always moving all the students who were not doing well academically into the same class for the school's afternoon prep period, while others whose academic performance were above average, would remain in their classes, manned by their class teachers. I was usually manning the class where all the below average students were seated for their afternoon prep periods with the school counselors. Once there was a marked improvement in their academics they would be moved back to their usual classes for the afternoon prep again.

The programme in the below average prep class was such that, a counseling talk of about 15mins on the topics like "you can make it" "steps to being a high achiever" "how to be focused" and "Mathematics Is simple." "Concentration and focus are really essential" etc. after which they would ask questions on the topic discussed. The next 20 minutes will be spent in reading through all the notes they had copied that day. The next 25mins will be spent in doing the assignments given to them in their various classes by their teachers. Once the time for prep was up, they were expected to complete the remaining assignment at home.

However, we would have ensured that they had read in a focused manner during that prep period.

I would usually take my seat in a corner around the prep room environment to counsel them, one after the other. At that time it was a schedule of about 20mins per student, apart from seeing them at break time (after they might have had their lunch) and other free periods until the problems were solved concerning each of them, after which a better academic performance would ensue. The face of the child would have become charming and radiant and he would then be full of life again. This exercise afforded me the opportunity of getting the information I am divulging to you in this book. If I was not bothered about the plight of my students then I would not have had the privilege of assisting them to get reformed. I really felt fulfilled doing it because they were encouraging results emanating from the efforts I was putting into it.

So, one of such prep periods, I decided to call Jenkins, to interrogate him and know what his problems were that affected his focus, concentration and performance in class, which might soon affect his behavior if nothing was promptly done.

He said he did not know his father, he had never met him before but he was told by his uncle with whom he was living then, that he resided in Canada with his wife and children . Incidentally, the mother just had him for his father but they never got married. As at that time he was living with his father's junior brother who was himself married with children .

He continued by saying that, he was living with his mother since he was born, until he was ten years. One Saturday morning, his uncle came to take him away from his mum to his own house, where he had lived for three years as at then. The mum too was already married with three children for her husband and Jenkin was also living with them. He said he was enjoying his stay there. He said that he felt dejected and totally downcast as if the whole world had collapsed on him after he moved to his uncle's house, especially after they stopped his mother from visiting him. Three years after the incident, he had not recovered from the hard blow and he was totally helpless about it. He started weeping as he was telling me. I counseled him and arranged some counseling therapy for him and he got stabilized and picked up again.

Time and space will not permit me to enumerate the counseling procedure and therapy he was given but my joy about his case was that he became normal again and started performing well academically and he became focused again while life became meaningful to him, all over again.

I did not invite his mum or uncle to get him settled, In his own situation, if his uncle was invited, he will hate him for it and he will suffer for divulging such a story to us, in school.

My main point of writing these stories is for single parents to know that the children can have some challenges too, despite whatever provision you make available for them at home as the parent. Jenkins uncle was providing everything for him at home as confessed by the boy to me. As at that time, he was attending a very expensive high brow school which would certainly be the envy of many of his peers who did not have the opportunity he had, but there was still a problem he was confronting and which could thwart his destiny, if it was not solved in a good time.

Permit me to mention here that challenges might not be peculiar to children from single parents home only, but they are more prone to having it. As a matter of fact, 80% of the children I counseled out of some challenges of life, who found their feet back again and progressed thereby were from single parent homes.

4. The case of Samuel Amon, an eleven years old boy was another case in point. The parents had only him, but they were separated. The mother was based in Germany while the father was a business man in Nigeria who was a car dealer and a hotelier. The father came in to collect the form of the school for him in the company of a friend of his who also collected a form for his son. The children were both admitted into the school and they were in the same class.

   The school was not informed that the parents were separated. I just observed that Samuel's parents were usually sitting together with him on visiting days while the father's friend and his wife would sit together with their own child.

   After the first session, I stopped seeing Samuel's father on visiting days. I also observed that Samuel had stopped coming to school. On interrogation, the friend to Samuel's father, told me that on the vacation day for the session, Samuel's mother who was domiciled in Germany, arrived before the father and took the boy away to Germany. She was said to have told the husband that the boy would henceforth be living with her in Germany. We were told that the boy was actually a German citizen. The parents got married in Germany, had him there before they divorced and the custody of the child had been a tussle between them.

   I can imagine what the boy will be going through emotionally. I just noticed that the boy was extremely quiet which was indeed, a distress sign in the life of any child

5. Another case that struck me to the marrow was that of Dunsin, a boy in the final year of a secondary school who had never sighted his father since he was born. The first time he saw his father was in my office. I felt surprised about the incident and how on earth such can

happen to a child. The mother had been the one visiting the school and paying his fees. She bore all his expenses and she was responsible for all the nurturing and care expected of a parent, over the child.

The mother was always there for him and the boy was doing well in his academics and very well behaved. The reason for his well being is not far-fetched; the mother had accepted her fate and was not distracted in bringing up her only child.

She told me the story herself that the father of the boy resided in England with his wife and children . He came home on a visit to Nigeria and pregnated her. She had not delivered the child when he went back to resume work in England and his entire family never knew that he had pregnated any lady in Nigeria.

She delivered the baby and had been nursing him all alone and raising him, paying his fees and discharging all the required parental duties all alone because she could not trace the man again, neither did she know any of his relatives. The man too did not tell anybody about it. She said ever since then she was always afraid to go into any love relationship with any man, because she was afraid of being jilted again. As a result of this unique experience of hers, she decided to be very close to the son and raise him up to be a real comfort to her in future. The boy's behavior even at seventeen reflected the picture of a highly responsible and well brought up young adult indeed.

She continued by saying that the boy kept on asking for his father. All the mother could show him was the picture she took with the father during her short interaction with him. The boy was bearing the name of his father.

The incessant disturbance of the mother by the boy led her to reflect one day about the matter and suddenly remembered that the "run-away" husband had a friend who could still be traced, he was always accompanying him to her house whenever he visited her, then.

She took her time to trace the man via the office where he was working then, down to where he could be found at the time of her investigation. She got the address, phone number and e-mail address of Dunsin's father in England. She followed it up through her sister who was resident in England. He was found at last and the picture of the child was sent to him showing every stage of his growth and development. He owned up that the boy was his son and he then mentioned the incident to his wife and children who were all married as at then (3 boys and a girl). They all embraced the boy and accepted him. They all started communicating with him. Dunsin's mother came to school to narrate the incident to me as the Principal of his son, especially as he was a boarder. She told me that she really prayed to God for His intervention, as a result of which the problem was solved.

The day Dunsin's father was to come and meet the son for the first time, my office was the chosen venue. I had already briefed him that he should prostrate fully on the floor before the father immediately he sees him so that the father can release a parental blessing on him which will rest on him forever because parental blessings are more potent than parental prayers, even though both are important and effective.

We all sat in my office i.e. Dunsin, the mum and I, waiting for the arrival of a father whom he had never seen before in his seventeen years of existence. Immediately he stepped in, Dunsin prostrated flat on his tummy before the father and true to my expectation he rained blessings on him after which Dunsin got up and they both hugged themselves (father and son) for a long time tears were rolling down our cheeks as we witnessed the unique incident.

Thank God for a prayerful and responsible single parent like Dunsin's mother, the boy's life might have been messed up. If it was not for God's intervention, the man might have denied his paternity of the boy or he might have treated the matter with levity; his wife and children might not have welcomed the "sudden addition to the family."

Dunsin's final year results were excellent. He even won a scholarship to a University in UK, for his desired course.

6. I used to have a student, Shola in one of the schools where I taught. As a teacher, I was in the habit of being close to my students so that I can nurture them appropriately like a mother to them, apart from being their teacher.

Shola was a half-cast, she was a very good girl, disciplined and brilliant but to my surprise, I met the parents at a parents dinner, organized by the school for interactive purposes and to my utmost surprise, they were both dark in complexion and clearly they were Africans. I asked her in the school the following day about why it was so? She said it was a long story.

I insisted on hearing the gist "that is the term the teenager will use in referring to that type of story I was demanding for".

She told me that her mother was a British Lady who was the father's girl friend when he was studying in a University in England. The relationship resulted into her birth, but they were never married, so, she was told by her father that with the permission of her mother, he brought her to Nigeria at 3 years old and the mother remained in Britain since then without any communication with him or her child. She said that when she was 14 years old, she demanded for her contact address, name and description of how to locate her, but the father refused to give it to her.

As at when she was telling me this, she was 16 years old and in the final year of a secondary school. She however made it clear to me that she had been well taken care of by her step mother and her father. Her father had two other children from the step mother who were both boys. She was highly loved by everyone in the family but she would still want to know her real mother and meet with her if she was still alive. I began to counsel her against being troubled about such a concern, especially as she was not suffering in any way.

Note that, I said she was well behaved and brilliant like Dunsin. In both cases, the available parents were committed to the nurturing of the children and their total well-being despite the situation of things. They didn't allow the matter to get worse by abandoning the children. They didn't allow the children's destiny to become thwarted. Single parent should learn from this.

Some years after, I met one of Shola's classmates in secondary school, as at then, most of the students in her set whom I taught were married. She was said to have got married too but, I was told that in her final year in the University which she attended in the United States, she came in contact with someone who knew the mother and the person gave her the mother's contact details. She traced her where about and found her. As at then, the mother had no other child. So it was a very happy reunion.

Some of these stories have been related to enable single parents know that no matter how loving, caring and supportive of your child you may be, he will still have the yearning, interest, desire of seeing and interacting with his absentee parent. It is psychological; there is nothing anybody can do about it. This does not mean that the child is not appreciative of your effort, care and love.

The human system has been wired like that by God. It is not the fault of such children. In most cases, no matter how negative you paint the picture of the absentee father or mother, the truth is that as teenagers, they will love him more than you and feel sorry for his unfortunate situation. Even if you don't want them to know, see or have any dealings with him, they will still bye pass you to see him, once they get to the position of helping him financially, they will do so. They will also care for you as well as the dear parent who rescued them. So, avoid being jealous if such a situation arises.

7. The case of Omolara was one that I will never forget. In fact, it is a very low self esteem, that is truncating her destiny till now. Her present state of life is such that God's intervention is urgently needed for her to settle back to life and be normal again.

The family confusion that is still affecting her now, even at 42 years old, started from the time she was 2'/, years old. Omolara's father was a Banker at the time she was born, while the mother was a semi-illiterate young lady and they were living happily together. When she was 2'/, years old, the father fell in love with a colleague of his in the Bank and they both decided to get married. This they did and he moved the new wife into their two bed-room flat where he was living with his first wife and only child then.

The father and the new wife were living in one of the two rooms of the two bedroom apartment, while Omolara and the mother were living in the second room. About 6 months after the new wife moved in, Omolara's mother suddenly ran mad one morning and she was taken to a native doctor in her village who was believed to be an expert in the treatment of psychiatric cases. Omolara was henceforth being taken care of by the father and step-mother. She grew up believing that her father's wife was her mum. The step mother had three children of her own, two girls and one boy.

Omolara said that when she became more matured, specifically at the age of twelve years old, she realized that the siblings enjoyed a measure of preferential treatment than herself with their mum. This aroused her curiosity to want to know why it was so. She found out that she was never able to satisfy her supposed mother, no matter what she did. She would also condemn all her actions, words and deeds and get punished for almost everything while her junior ones were always commended and exonerated. Her father, on the other hand, was always there for her.

When she became an undergraduate in a University in Nigeria, she met someone from her home town who was introduced to her by her roommate. His name was Gideon. They were also course mates. One day, after lecturers Gideon told her that he mentioned her name to his uncle who told him that Omolara's mother was related to his own parents. Omolara became curious as this would enable her to unravel her curiosity about her real parentage. On meeting with Gideon's uncle, she asked all her questions and they were all answered by him with full details, descriptions of events and dates attached. As a matter of fact, Gideon's uncle was living with Omolara's parents when all the incidents that led to the mother's insanity occurred.

It was through him that Omolara got to know that the mother had a mental problem and had to be taken to a native doctor in their village. Mr. Alli, Gideon's uncle offered to take Omolara there the following week, because as at the time of the discussion, it was 18 years after the incident, her mother was still mentally sick and she was still in the custody of Baba Adu, the native doctor.

On the agreed date, Mr. Alli Gideon's uncle took Omolara there. She was shocked to see her real mother in chains, looking tattered and unkempt. She couldn't recognize her daughter neither could they communicate at all because of her mental state.

Omolara was in a state of shock all through that day and several weeks and months after. She wept in secret uncontrollably that day and several times after. The father did not still disclose anything to her and she felt it will be odd for her to ask him a question that might sound foolish like "Daddy, Is Mama Bisi my real mother?" The way they interacted among themselves in her immediate family will not warrant such a question, except if an issue that might lead to it, but there was none. Everything seems to be going on smoothly among the children and parents in her immediate family but for the suspicion she felt within her. So she decided not to say anything about her discovery, neither did she mention to her father that she met her mum's relation, Mr. Alli.

Omolara got destabilized about the incident; she failed some compulsory courses that semester. She later decided to pick herself up again, cast her cares Jesus and encouraged herself in the Lord her God just as David did in the Bible.

She continued with her life but she made up her mind never to trust any man again in her life and it has affected her till today.

She decided to visit her mum about two months after. When she got there, she was told that her mother had died about two weeks after her visit. It was then revealed to her that she recovered from the illness but suffered a relapse thereafter which claimed her life.

The repercaution of this had serious negative effect on Omolara ever since, especially as it had to do with her love affairs with the opposite sex.

She went through her University education successfully but never had any lasting love relationship that resulted into marriage except for once, when she got married to an old school mate of hers, Tunde and the marriage lasted for only 8 months. After then, she was into a relationship with Ibukun, a church member of hers. They were in a serious courtship for three years after which they broke up. As at now she is 42 years old and yet unmarried. She has a very good job with a multinational company, where she occupies a managerial post.

The last time I heard of her from one of her school mates who gave me her phone number, I heard that she built a house in the outskirt of a village where she now lives alone. How will she be discovered by any man there for a marriage proposal?

8. A set of twins Jane and Jill were my students in one of the schools where I worked and I was very much in tune with all my students as their teacher and mother and sometimes their mum and dad.

Jane and Jill, were a set of female twins. As at the time of this incident, they were in the senior secondary three. They were 13years old then. They were always afraid of going home because of their temporary live-in-step fathers who was always harassing them sexually but secretly, without the knowledge of their mum.

They related their dilemma to me and I asked why they have not reported the matter to their mum. They said they were afraid to mention it to her.

In the process, they reported to me one day that the live-in-step father (their mother's lover) had left due to a misunderstanding between him and their mum. They were secretly happy but they didn't allow their mum to know. Within about 8 months (because I was counting it) they had three live-in-fathers (i.e. their mum's lovers) living with them at one time or the other.

They hated their mother for it and yearned to go and live with their father who had already remarried with about four children. They were always wishing to go and live with their father and half siblings. They were communicating with them amicably without their mother's knowledge.

I am sure that once they leave the house for a University environment, they will have the time and freedom to link up fully with their father and half siblings just like all the others like them, that I knew. They always say nice things about them.

Meanwhile, their mother had given us a standing instruction not to allow their father to visit them. We did just that and the children were emotionally disturbed, though. However, he still had a way of communicating with them.

As a single parent, remember that the children are bound to love both parents. It is psychological. Nobody can help it. If you want them to hate the other parent just because you are separated or that you are the only one bearing the cost of their upbringing, it will affect them emotionally and their destinies can be affected. So please, let them live normally.

Despite the fact that something had gone wrong with the relationship, the children should not be brought into the confusion. It is advisable that you assist them in growing up normally like other children, in your own interest.

Chapter 16

Tips That Could Guide You The Single Parent of a
Teenager

God has not ordained that parenting responsibilities should be discharged by one of the two parents because of the enormous duties and activities involved in it e.g.

(a) Too many decisions taken by the only parent available without consultation with anybody.

(b) Too many duties to be carried out at home by only one parent, this will no doubt get the single parent stressful, worn out and disillusioned.

(c) Only one person will be faced with several expenses incurred on the child or children as the case may be.

Despite all these, please, be aware that if a single parent is not vigilant enough and fully committed to his/her parenting responsibilities, the adverse effect can be more frustrating.

Possible negative reaction of a teenager from a negligent single parent home.

1. Early involvement in sexual activity

Research had shown that most teenage children of single mothers exhibit lower moral standard than those living with both biological parents. It has also being confirmed through research that most girls in single parent homes are at a more greater risk engaging in early sexual activities, teenage marriage, teenage pregnancy, non- marital birth and divorce than girls in normal families.

Undergraduate students with divorced parents have been found to be more sexually active than their course mates from intact homes. This is especially true of male children from divorced homes. They tend to enjoy "recreational sex" than a committed relationship and in most cases, they are prone to have had several sex partners before graduation.

The reason for their active sexual lives (both males and females) among them is that in some cases, single parents forget that their children are watching them, especially their teenage ones, so in an attempt to re-marry or go on with life sexually, they feel justified to have sexual partners anyhow, without taking cognizance of the fact that by so doing, they are introducing their children to such a sexually free life as well. They usually feel justified about it, being oblivious of the damage they are doing to the morals of their children.

In some cases, single parents have live-in-lovers who also have regular sexual relationship with their teenage children without their knowledge, like the case of Jane and Jill, the twin whose case I narrated to you in a previous chapter.

The pity is that once these children start off with early sexual activities engendered by the dilemma they have found themselves in, they usually find it difficult to stop.

How I wish we have stable homes in order to prevent our teenage children from such a calamity.

However, I hereby appeal to single parents to ensure that they stand as real role models to their children.

Nobody prayed to be a single parent from the onset. It occurred due to some uncontrollable situations beyond the control of the individual. I would have thought that the knowledge of the possible effect of such an action on their children should bring about a change in behavior on the part of such parents in the interest of the children.

A story about a boy, Innocent in the Senior Secondary School Two Class

He was 14 years old then. He was a boarder who got born again in school and was actually one of the Fellowship leaders in the school's fellowship. He was one of our vibrant student ministers in the school.

I noticed that Innocent was always looking frightened and sad whenever it was time to go home on holidays, mid-term break or end of term break when all the other students will be happy to go home. I was always ignoring such gesture until one Saturday morning when I visited the dormitory around 7:00am during the morning prep, shortly before the hostel cleaning exercise by the boarders.

I saw Innocent, a very tall boy, weeping profusely, all alone in one corner. I went to him and he was surprised to see me, he started wiping the tears on his face. I took him to my office and we sat down to talk.

He confided in me that the parent divorced when he was eight years old and at the time of this incident being reported here, he was 14 years old. He continued by informing me that the father did not re-marry but he has been bringing different ladies home as temporary wives to live with them. He had two siblings who were girls. The girls were living with their mum while he was living with their dad.

His fear was that he was not sure of the temperament of the lady who had just moved in with hisfather immediately he left home for school early that term. His experience had been that some of the ladies turn out to be kind and loving in their relationship with him when others might be so hostile and negligent of him.

He recounted his experience with one of them, Jumoke who was so negligent that he was not usually served with any meal whenever his father was not around. In some cases, he would only eat once a day. He added that the rule was that they must not be reported to his dad otherwise he will suffer the more. He said Jumoke's love relationship with his dad only lasted for nine months and she was the only one who stayed longest with his dad. The love duration of each live-in-lover with his dad, according to him was usually 4-6 months maximum.

Many of our teenagers, both boys and girls go through the same problem hence, the possibility of being promiscuous is high. In some cases such live-in-mothers force the boys to bed with them.

Thank God for Innocent who said he refused such love advances from one of his father's live-in-wives who moved into their house during a summer break when the father went on an official trip to France. He said he refused to go to bed with her. He refused to the end and damned all consequences because according to him, he would not want to offend God and go to hell.

Thank God that he was born again in school and he has listened to several preachings on the assembly, class fellowship, dormitory morning and night devotion and Sunday services, otherwise, his life would have become ruined by the virtue of such immoral circumstances he found himself.

He said he reported the matter to his father's friend who was also his colleague, who intervened and moved him to his house in the interim. When the father returned from his trip, he ejected the lady and ended the relationship with her immediately.

Alas, many other children like Innocent still suffer from such situations today.

2. Academic Problem:

Due to negligent of parenting duties which is prevalent in single parents homes (where their parents are careless) than intact homes, many of them score lower grades in their school examinations and tests.

The reasons are that
i. It is more difficult for children to concentrate on school work in times of family crisis.

ii. Scoring lower grades by them may be a means of gaining attention or it might be a way of expressing rebellion.

iii. Some single parents behave indecently and their children resent it. This could get the child distracted.

3. Behavioural Problems:

Some children exhibit behavioural problems in the wake of their parent's separation or divorce. They may start missing school. They may suddenly have problems getting along with others. They may become disrespectful. This is an expression of anger, confusion or a response to emotional turmoil which they feel inwards but they find it difficult to express it in words.

POSSIBLE PSYCHOLOGICAL AND EMOTIONAL STATE OF A TEENAGER FROM A SINGLE PARENT HOME.

The effects should be cushioned by the available parent so that the child can be an achiever, indeed.

In single parents homes where the available partner is focused, determined to get it right with the children, leads by example and amiable with the children, they will grow up to be matured and free from almost all the perceived effects that others in their shoes suffer.

Whatever the circumstances are that led to the occurrence of a single parent home, whether the death of a parent, divorce, separation, desertion, abdication of responsibilities (even when the parents live together in the same house) to a partner, transfer etc.

The following are some of the effects that are likely to be felt by a teenage or adolescent child from such a background.

(a) **Shame or Embarrassment**
These are commonly felt by most teenagers from single parents homes because of the perceived situation of their families. They interpret the situation as an indication of an anomaly in their family settings. They have a feeling of embarrassment by what they consider as an inappropriate conduct on the part of their parents following the divorce, especially where mum and dad are dating another man or woman respectively. It could also be because of a probable change in their standard of living after the occurrence that led to a single parent home e.g. smaller apartment; transfer to a less expensive school, etc.

(b) **Guilt**
In some cases, such children assume blame or at least part of it, for the failure of their parents' relationship, especially if it occurred in their presence and all the issues that led to it, were to their knowledge.

Majority of them suffer from a feeling of utter helplessness, but they will hardly discuss it at home especially with the available parent, because they are already pitying her for the heavy load meant for two people, which she is carrying alone. They will be prepared to co-operate with her for the success of the home in general and the children in particular as long as she "behaves well" and she is disciplined, if not, it will be difficult for her to control the children..

(c) **Rejection**
This is one of the deepest feelings such children experience, even in a situation where the single parent is doing his/her best. The sense of rejection may still persist, emotionally.

(d) **Anger**
In the midst of their confusion, they sometimes feel angry about the situation they have found themselves. Those who lost a parent feel angry, believing that they have been cheated and deprived by nature of the support and love of the dead parent. In cases of divorce, separation, negligence (i.e. where the parents both live together but one had abandoned all parental responsibilities to the other) or desertion the teenage child will experience anger towards the parent who left, especially after hearing different negative stories about him or her, but at the same time he/ she will pity his situation.

If a part of the story getting to the child indicates insufficiency, suffering or incapability to make ends meet on the part of the absentee parent, the child will love him more and pity his situation. He will be ready to help him out to attain the right status, if possible. In some cases, where the various stories they have heard indicated that the available parent was at fault, especially if he was adjudged by the child as indisciplined at that moment, the child will hate him/her and vent his anger of him/her by way of being disobedient and incorrigible

(e) **Insecurity/unhealthy self esteem**
Teenagers in such families may be especially vulnerable to feeling of insecurity and low self-esteem. The circumstances that led to the divorce or separation process itself and the condition that commonly follow a divorce/ separation often affect the children's sense of worth. They feel different and they usually believe that

their parents took such a decision irrespective of their well-being because they were considered worthless to them. They feel inferior to children from intact families. In some cases, they feel stigmatized by their church members, classmates, teachers neighbours, especially in Africa where many people still frown at divorce and separation. It is believed to be a westernized way of life.

Stigmatization might also occur because of a single parent's bahaviour e.g. parents engaging in alcoholism, promiscuity and several other indecent ways of life exhibiting indiscipline and lack of control.

It can strike a creeping blow on the hardship already faced by the child and result into a low self esteem.

CONCLUSION

I want to repeat here again that in a situation where the single parent who has enough time for the child, parent him carefully, committed, leads him by example, monitor his school work and his social life, praise him when necessary and also scolds him whenever he deserves to be scolded, implements all that has been stated in this book for a successful teenage parenting, the repercussion of single parenthood will be minimized to the barest minimum in such children. They will not have too many problems as I have enumerated.

The purpose of itemizing all that had been written in this book about how single parenting can affect a teenage child adversely is to enable parents who are carrying out this Divine duty all alone to be aware of the possible consequences of the situation on their children, if they act otherwise.

In most cases, single parents always believe that their children don't have any problem emanating from that unexpected status as long as they are provided with all the good things of life which their mates enjoy. They go through some psychological trauma that they don't discuss with anybody except those who show enough interest in their welfare and whom they can trust with their secret.

Chapter 17

Relating with Teenagers from Single Parent Homes by their Parents

(a) Bevery close to them:
Always interact intimately with them. See them as not just your children but also your friend in the real sense of the word.

(b) Only allow disciplined people to live with you, otherwise they might influence them negatively. Beware of allowing those you can't vouch for, into your house to live with you.

(c) Perform your parental duties extremely well as you ought to, so that you don't worsen the situation by allowing them to become in disciplined and useless, depending on you for everything forever, running into one trouble or the other, ending up biting your ears for not bringing them up adequately. What will be your excuse? The fact that a child is from a single parent home, is not an excuse to be unsuccessful. Several others like him are doing well with the support of focused and responsible single parents. The renowned Doctor, Ben Carson is a product of a single parent home and there are several others like them all over the world.

(d) Don't say negative things about the absentee parents in their presence. They will pretend that they are not missing him because you are still the one feeding, housing, clothing them and paying their school fees. Instead of that, talk to God about any challenge you have. He is the only one who can solve our problems by giving you the directives of how to go about applying the required solutions for peace of mind and tranquility. God was the one who ordained marriage in the Garden of Eden. He was the One who said that it was not good for the man to be alone. So cast all your cares on Him alone, I can assure you that He will sort you out. Don't cast your cares on the children. They cannot sort you out; it will only weigh them down and get them distracted, as you would have seen in the stories I had narrated.

(e) Don't feel cheated that you have been the only one raising the children alone, and that later the absentee parent will show up and enjoy the fruit of your labour, instead of you enjoying it alone. Remember that God is the One who has been providing all you have been spending on the children. The Bible tells us that, children are his heritage. They belong to Him. God will ensure that you do not lack any good thing and you will never suffer, as you play your parental roles diligently. God will make sure that you don't have a better last year; that your life will continue to be radiant and fulfilling. It will be difficult for you to explain why God has decided to decorate your life with His beauty and glory. It is simply because you are actively involved in His creative process, because after you have nurtured the children well, they will leave home as matured, disciplined, dependable individual to go and start off their respective families, thereby extending God's divine creative processes on a wider dimension.

(f) Repeat regularly to your children, if they are missing their father that God is the Father of each individual, apart from our earthly father. Once we establish a true relationship with Him by giving our lives to Jesus, allowing the Holy Spirit to lead us on daily basis, reading our Bibles daily, obeying its content and talking to God our Father everyday and everywhere, we are safe and secured forever. Let them know that, it is the only way to true success, great achievement and complete fulfillment.

(g) Always pray with them and release blessings on them every day. Keep repeating to them, whatever you want to see in their lives now and in the future, I can assure you that it will be so, because you are an authority figure in their lives.

As parents, God has given us the responsibility to nurture them, so he has added authority to it, that will enable us to accomplish our divine assignment on them with ease, because one day, we will stand before Him to give an account of our parental duties over our children. So be focused, and ensure that you do it successfully, despite all odds.

(h) It is very essential for you to be a role model to your children. Whatever you are discouraging them from doing as indecent, must not be practiced by you too. Teenagers believe in "Do as I do" not "Do as I say"only.

(i) Believe in them and let them know it. They will develop the right self esteem for achievers.So:-

(j) Let your teenage children know that there are certain things we cannot change as human beings. We just must live with such things and make the best of such a situation for a better future, as we surrender such to God and believe in Him, that He is able to see us through

MY APPEAL

My appeal to you as a single parent is to apply all that had been outlined in all the chapters of this book including this specified chapter for "Single Parents"

God will raise the children with you in Jesus' name especially as they belong to Him. Develop the "I can do it" spirit instead of looking down on yourself and feeling helpless and dejected.

(k) G) Always listen to them no matter what they are trying to express and give them concrete and honest answers. Take time to explain any issue to them the way they are. One can't easily lie to a teenager because they are very intelligent but many adults don't know this. So, they simply look down on them as young. They know a lot, much more than many adults. They just keep quiet around adults who don't believe they are children. Once you believe in them and let them know you will see and enjoy the genius and the giant in them.

(l) G) Make sure that you don't lament before them or wear a feeling of sorrow or look downcast, because it will affect their emotions negatively and consequently their studies in general. Rather, do it behind them. Have a mentor, who had successfully gone through what you are going through now for advice and also discuss your feelings with God on such an occasion. The Holy Spirit will comfort you, if you have given your life to Christ and lead you through successfully. He will let you know the right steps to take per time.

(m) Make sure that they have good relationship with God individually. It will enhance their lives through the situation with ease until they grow up as matured, responsible and successful men and women or until the situation becomes normal again. Either way, they will sail through with ease.

God will congratulate you for a job well done, when you stand before him on the last day.

GOD REPLENISHES YOUR POCKETS
As for the only parent responsible for picking the bills of the home, God will always empower you financially to do it, because they are His children.

Assignment
Check every family you can have an access to and find out who it is that is picking all the bills of the family and meeting every need of that family as well?

I have conducted such a research some time ago, my findings are:

My Findings on the research:

The one who picks the bill of each family is the one who will be getting richer while the other person who might think he is smart by dodging the required parental responsibilities and sponsorship of the needs of the children will continue to get poorer. He will always lack money and continue to live in penury, except he turns a new leaf and rise up to his responsibilities.

The secret is that God is the one who provides for all the needs of each family and He directs the money into the purses, pockets and accounts of the parent who is responsible for the upkeep of the home.

So, don't feel cheated if you are a single parent doing it all alone. God will continuously replenish your purse, pockets and accounts.

Don't worry, you will never lack any good thing. **JUST GET WELL CONNECTED TO GOD ALWAYS** and He will never leave you or forsake you. **HE NEVER DISAPPOINTS ANYONE WHO TRUSTS IN HIM!!!**

Chapter ⑱

Teenagers
Can be Amazingly
Extra-ordinary,
If Given the Chance

As parents and adults around them, many of us miss the tremendous opportunity which we would have had as a result of the privilege of having them around us, because we under rate their abilities.

It has always been so, since ancient times, till now.

They Have The "I Can Do It" Spirit

Teenagers believe that they can do anything positive. It reminds me of the story of David in the Bible. He was also a teenager at the time he was under-rated by the father. When Samuel the Prophet was commissioned to go and anoint the next king of Israel, among the children of Jesse of Bethlehem.

When he got to Jesse's house, he made the intention of God known to him. Jesse brought out all his children except David whom he regarded as too young for the exercise. At the end of the day, he was the one considered eligible to be anointed as king.

The same thing happened when Goliath of Gath, a Philistine was taunting the army of Israel at the battle front and nobody was able to take up the challenge and go up to where he was standing. He challenged them continuously for a fight with him, if they were sure of the power of their God. They were all afraid to face him except the young David who was not even a member of the Armed Forces of Israel. He was just a young boy whose responsibility at home was to take care of the sheep of his father and probably to do other menial chores. No one knew that he was so intimate with God in the process of carrying out his assigned duty of a shepherd. He had learnt to trust God absolutely and God had promised us in the Bible that anyone who puts his trust in Him will never be ashamed. It is also recorded in the Bible that "woe betides he who puts his trust in man." David had tested and proved God, as infallible, ever faithful and ever true. Whatever God has said He will do,

He will surely get it accomplished, as long as we believe in it and play our human part in the matter. Is it not surprising that even at that young age, David knew what his senior brothers did not know about God. So, don't under rate your teenage children, they are capable of doing exploits, even much more than David did, especially as they are living in a more technological age than David, if only we can believe in them and let them know that we do, they will surprise us, much more than David did in his own time.

David's senior brother, Eliab felt David was being foolish or childish by being confident enough to volunteer himself for the confrontational one-on-one battle with the giant Goliath, who was an experienced soldier with sophisticated weapons of war in his possession, for the encounter. King Saul did not expect such a young boy to be able to fight against Goliath, so he tried to discourage David from going up to fight with Goliath, whom king Saul considered as superior to David on the battle field. David insisted, so king Saul decided to equip him with a protective iron jacket against any missile from Goliath, but as young as David was, he knew what he was doing much more than the adults around him were aware of.

He first accepted the protective jacket and gadgets given to him by the king and he wore them as prescribed probably some on the head, body, legs and toes. This hindered his movement; he removed and returned them back to the king. He said to the king that "The Lord who delivered me from the paw of the lion and the paw of the bear will deliver me from the hand of this Philistine." King Saul said to him immediately "Go, and the Lord will be with you" and David went and won the battle.

Don't forget that he just came to the battle field to give his brothers who were considered old enough to be in the army, some food, probably packed in a food flask from home.

He killed Goliath in a confrontational battle not with any sophisticated weapon but simply with his shepherd staff and five smooth stones picked from the stream. After he killed Goliath, he cut off his head and handed it over to the king, to the amazement and appreciation of all. Joseph too, had a dream about his ultimate life from God as a teenager and he pursued it to a conclusive end, despite all odds and the dream came to pass.

Our teenagers have the "I can do it" spirit in them, let them exercise it. Don't under rate them, otherwise, they will not be able to exercise their prowess and superfluous God-given ability. If David was not given the chance to fight against Goliath eventually, Israel would not have won the battle on that day. It is the same thing with our teenage children. At times their ideas or proffered solutions to problems might sound too childish and unreasonable, but still give them the chance to test it out as long as the consequences are not injurious, if he fails to achieve his aim, at least it would have been a very good way to practice and next time he will perform better.

So, let's give them the chance to behave, reason and act like adults. Let's believe in them and let them know it. It will enable them to think fast and more intelligently than when we keep seeing them like children. The teenage age is a period of training them for the attainment of adulthood which they are about to graduate into. If we allow them to assume the adult position in time, as adolescents, they will easily become great achievers early in life.

In my country, Nigeria and in several other countries of the world, history had shown that we had (I am sure we will still be having such in some parts of the world today), young men and women between twenty-six and twenty-eight years old who had occupied the political positions of Head of State,

President of the nation, Ministers and Commissioners. Several others at that age had become worldwide renowned achievers in one way or the other. I believe very strongly that they must have been handled by parents and adults who believed in them, which must have encouraged them to do exploit when they were younger. So, if we handle them like children, they will eventually believe they are children and behave as such. Several teenagers in history and even, in contemporary times, had done remarkable things and they are still influencing the cause of history positively, because the adults who brought them up, developed the "I can do it" spirit in them, hence they are doing exploits today.

They Can Be Multi-Talented
Teenagers have the ability of being multi-talented like David was. He was a shepherd, a warrior and an excellent musician. So, observe in him what his talents are likely to be. Encourage him to develop it. Give him all the support he requires to be a great achiever in the area of his strength and you will see him soaring higher and higher in such fields of endeavour, as you patiently assist him to overcome his weaknesses. Intimacy with him and regular dialogue, will do it

They Are Multi-Tasked
They are capable of doing many things together at a time and make a success of each of them, with your permission, however they must be guided against loosing focus on their academic work; otherwise, many of them have the tendency of being carried away with such things, at the detriment of their academic work, if not properly guided.

Don't Take Them For Granted
They can be very wise and intelligent. They can't easily be deceived and you can't hide anything from them as adults because, they are wiser than we think. If you give them the chance to advice you on any issue, you will be shocked at the

dexterity with which they will do it. They will not draw their examples from national occurrences alone, but also from the international ones, with facts and figures, courtesy, the media and modern technology. Many of us adults are not even conversant with modem technology as they are, however, once they have been properly brought up, they will not be affected by the negative effect of these new technological development.

Once you start allowing him/her to start advising you and if you take the advice, it will enable you to advice him/her too, with ease and with the required response, whenever there is a need for it. It is a good way of bonding with them. Let us know as adults that they can't be taken for granted, because they read in between the lines to decipher what you mean by every sentence you utter; every situation that seems clouded and every action of the adults around them, to check you out and be sure of what is going on really.

They Like To Be Respected
If they are respected by the adults around them, they will appreciate and ensure that they don't misbehave in any way to such an adult so as not to lose it. They will make sure that they don't disappoint you and live up to expectation by all means.

To respect them does not indicate that you kneel down or prostrate to greet them or refer to them as "Sir or Ma" but rather, it is all about choosing your words when you address them and don't treat them like children. Simply relate with them and address them the way you will do to your colleagues and friends, irrespective of their age.

They Hate Being Embarrassed
They don't like to be embarrassed especially in the public or among the young ones or their peers. So they avoid doing anything that could lead to any embarrassment from their

parents or any adult around them. They avoid anyone who is always in the habit of embarrassing them. They prefer to be corrected or scolded in secret and in a friendly and respectful manner. They will make sure they take to your advice and they will avoid such a bad act henceforth.

Teenagers Can Be Excellent Goal-getters
If they have been given a very good upbringing with an adequate intimacy with their parents and the adults around them, who believe strongly in their abilities to succeed in whatever they lay their hands on, and if they let them know that they believe in their prowess and abilities without any doubt, they will be prepared to reach out for the moon and they will succeed.

Once you don't believe in them, they can easily write themselves off. So, you have the key to their success in your hands as parents in this regards, so use it and they will succeed.

Let him know your dos and don'ts as I have mentioned in an earlier chapter and be all out to ensure that you point out such faults or mistakes in a one on one manner showing that you trust and that he wouldn't have done it deliberately. He will endeavour to please you always and by so doing, developing the habit of high moral discipline and integrity.

CONCLUSION
As parents/ guardians, teachers and all other adults around them, let us spare the time now in pleasure so that we don't end up sparing the time in pain. Definitely the period of assessment will come when the good behavior or bad behavior of our teenage children will be clearly manifested. It will either bring grief or joy depending on how well we have been able to bring up the child. If you want to compel them to do the right thing during the upper teenage years, i.e. between ages of 17- 19 years old, they will rebel violently, especially if

you have not been accepted as a friend by them. At that age the child will likely still be an undergraduate in a higher institution or in some cases, he would have graduated. This is why we have the stories of children who brutally killed their parents, especially as they would have become drug addicts and cult members as at then, because of the neglect.

The story we all heard when we were growing up about the young man (who was most likely a teenager) who had to face the firing squad for a criminal offence he committed, that attracted a death penalty, how he took permission to have a dialogue with his mother, before his death. His request was granted. As the mother stepped forward and stood before him for the dialogue, he requested to whisper whatever he had to tell her, into her ear, so that nobody else would hear. As the mother turned her ear towards his mouth at a very close range, he bit off the ear of the mother. He shouted immediately after that he only rewarded her for her wickedness in not giving him, the right instruction of life, expected of parents, which would have enabled him to grow up to be a responsible and disciplined individual, which undoubtedly would have prevented him from being a criminal.

Let us all learn from this, as parents of teenage children. The story is very pertinent today to dissuade us from neglecting our parental duties for any reason under the sun. it should not be abdicated or contracted out to others, so that we don't live a life of regret later.

A Yoruba proverb states that "A child who is not well built and nurtured by the parents, will end up selling all the houses they have built."

It is our prayer that we do not experience this. So, let us rise up to the challenge as parents!!!

God will grant us the willingness, wisdom and ability to discharge this responsibility committed into our hands by Him.

We should be aware of the fact that we shall one day, stand before God to give an account of how well we have discharged the responsibility of caring for and nurturing the children he has assigned to our respective families. No excuse for non- performance, abandonment or negligence will be tenable before Him on that day.

So ensure that you work towards commendation from our Creator and not condemnation. Now is the time to work assiduously for a peaceful old age on earth and commendation before God in heaven, as we take care of these "Jewels of inestimable value" committed to our care by our loving Father

- God Almighty Himself.

ABOUT THE AUTHOR

Dr(Mrs) Funmi Oboye is an astute Educationist. She holds a B.Ed, M.Ed and a Ph.D Degree. She has been in the education sector for over three decades now, immediately after her first degree. She has been consistently involved in the parenting of teenage children, even till now, especially in all the secondary schools where she had worked.

She is of the opinion that teenagers as young adults have their own unique world where only adults who are believed to understand them are allowed in, otherwise they see every adult as oppressive, until they are proved wrong. She would always say that she had found teenagers very pleasant and interesting as" Adults-in-Training."

Her love for them had propelled her to insist on working in any environment where they could be found. This had been basically in secondary schools, hence she taught at Federal Government College, Ijanikin, Lagos; University of Lagos International School, Akoka, Lagos; Queen's College, Yaba, Lagos.

She also worked at the Federal Ministry of Education, Victoria Island Lagos, at the Bilateral Agreements, Commonwealth and African Affairs Division of the Ministry, after which she retired voluntarily from the Federal Civil Service.

She had also served in the capacity of a Vice-Principal, Principal and Educational Administrator in some reputable Private Secondary Schools.

She is an Educational Consultant Timray Educational Consult. Founder and President of Engr. Timothy, Tonloju Adesubokan Memorial Foundation for the under-priviledged women and children. An NGO which she named after her late father who was a philanthropist. She is an alumnus of the Lagos Business School, of the PAN-Africa University.

Her passion for excellence in the education sector of her beloved country, Nigeria, led her to author some books for teachers, by way of mentoring them, as well as other teachers all over the world i.e.

(a) Teachers' World Book 1
(b) Teachers' World Book 2
(c) Achieving Excellence As A Teacher
(d) The UniquenessOfTheTeachingProfession

Also, having observed that many parents relegate their parental duties to the background and focus on their jobs or businesses at the detriment of the actualization of the destinies of their children in particular and the well-being of the nation in general, she decided to put her parenting ideas in books for parents who care, to read and know how to go about raising responsible and God-fearing children who will not only be there for them in their old age, but also be useful to God and humanity. The books are:-

(a) MANAGING YOUR CHILD FOR EXCELLENCE. It contained general parenting principles that have assisted several parents in carrying out their parenting duties/obligations the right way, ever since it has been published. It has been in high demand nationally and internationally, to the glory of God.

The parenting of teenagers is a unique one because, it is a period when they are being coached to become adults. The training must be of a higher quality. So they have to be well interacted with, by their parents and all the adults around them in a peculiar manner. The need to announce this to the world, gave rise to the writing of this second book for parents, i.e. **"PARENTING A TEENAGER"**

She is married to Engr. Olaitan Oboye and they are blessed with lovely children viz - Foluso, Femi, Tolu, Toni and some grand children.

Books Authored by Dr. Funmi Oboye

FOR TEACHERS

1. Teachers World Book 1
2. Teachers World Book 2
3. The Uniqueness of the Teaching Profession
4. Achieving Excellence as a Teacher

FOR PARENTS/TEACHERS

5. Managing Your Child for Excellence
6. Parenting a Teenager

www.ingramcontent.com/pod-product-compliance
Lightning Source LLC
LaVergne TN
LVHW051836080426
835512LV00018B/2917